# CHEERS TO
# BASEBALL

# CHEERS TO
# BASEBALL

My Crazy 30-Year Journey in College Baseball:
Perseverance, Leadership and Unbelievable Stories

**DARREN MUNNS**

*atmosphere press*

To Sarah
For your incredible support

To Mary Ellen
For keeping the tough losses in perspective

*Art by Paul Sullivan*

# Table of Contents

# Foreword
## By Anne Rogers

As I look around my home office, my eyes shift to my right and settle on a row of baseballs. There are five of them, all sporting scuff marks and dirt from the baseball stadium they called home until they made their way to me in the press box, where I was stationed comfortably until a white blur came flying at me and I had to get out of the way. Four of these baseballs are from Major League Baseball stadiums spanning the time I have been a beat reporter for MLB.com. The first one is different!

The Columbia College logo appears on one side, the words, "Columbia College 2017 Home Opener" on another. I picked it up at the first Columbia College game I attended and is just as special as the other baseballs because it's where I got my first taste covering baseball. It was spring of 2017, and I was in my first semester covering a beat for the *Columbia Missourian,* a newspaper housed in the Missouri School of Journalism that covers the Columbia community. I was assigned to Columbia College and learned that I would be covering the school's first baseball team in 35 years. What a story that was -- and what a story for a first-time journalist.

The first thing I knew I had to do ahead of the home opener was meet the head coach. I met Darren Munns at the Columbia College basketball court, where we sat on the bleachers and talked about his newly built program, what the challenges of building it were and how excited he was to get this thing going, given he had been working on it for over a year. The first time I *really* met Darren, in his natural element, was on a freezing day at Atkins Park, when Columbia College played in front of its home fans against Williams Baptist College. I was not properly dressed for the windy April weather, but nevertheless, I settled into the metal bleachers with my homemade scorebook and watched the game.

The Cougars won, 16-5, and before I could ask Darren anything afterward, he gave me a hard time about not wearing a coat. And then he broke down why he thought that 2017 team was so special.

"I wanted highly competitive players but high in character as well. Once we finally got them together, it's pushing them every day and trying to be the best we can be. You recruit high-character guys and that enhances team chemistry because you get good players who are also good people. You get a step ahead of team chemistry before they even get there." To me, this quote was better than any one I got about the actual game. It provided me insight and context into who Darren is as a coach and leader, and what he values as he chases down wins and builds strong programs. This is why Columbia College's former athletic director Bob Burchard hired Munns to build this program from the ground up. It's why Munns' players bought into coming to a new program like Columbia College. It's why every aspiring coach or leader, in general, should read this book.

It's also why Munns is so qualified to write this book you're about to read -- and why you're about to enjoy it as much as I did. I think part of the reason I remember that semester so fondly, and why I keep that baseball on my desk, is because of the people I encountered, starting with Darren. He never denied a question I had, always made sure I got who I needed after games, and helped me thrive that semester, which ultimately landed me more journalism opportunities. If there is one thing I have learned since I started writing about sports, it's this: Sports always teach us something. The game teaches, sure, but mostly I'm talking about the people who hand down lessons as we watch them compete or coach or take over a behind-the-scenes role in their sport. Everyone has a story, and perhaps through theirs, we steal glimpses of our own.

Darren's story is one everyone should know and illustrates how hard work, dedication, and a refusal to give up can lead to tremendous success. That's true not only in his career but in also writing this book; when Darren called me in the early days of the 2020 coronavirus pandemic to say he was writing a book, all I could do was smile because I knew he would do it. The real takeaway from this book is that Darren has accomplished all of these things with the utmost class and integrity, while never losing sight of his passion and the reason he started coaching. Because I know he won't say it, I'll say it here: Cheers to Darren!

**Anne Rogers** covered the Columbia College baseball program in 2017 while she was a student at the University of Missouri. She graduated from the Missouri School of Journalism in 2019, and now covers the Kansas City Royals for MLB.com as a beat writer.

# Introduction

I have coached college baseball for nearly three decades, but in reality, Baseball has coached me. Leadership is defined as the action of leading a group of people or organization, and the word itself invokes positive connotations. However, leaders are influential for the entire range of results; positive, average, and negative. Teams finish in first place, teams finish with a .500 record, and teams finish dead last. Companies are Fortune 500, companies exist in neutral, and companies are quickly bankrupt. The term "natural born leader" is used frequently and is a testament to one's leadership abilities. There is truth to being an inherent leader as the term literally suggests, but life's experiences also provide an ongoing education in leadership. *Cheers to Baseball* is split into two sections. The first four chapters are an autobiographical account of sacrifices, experiences, and good times during my crazy thirty-year journey as a college baseball coach. The final seven chapters detail my most critical keys to leadership learned during those thirty years.

There are four avenues to becoming a head baseball coach at the college level. The first one is nepotism. Being the son of a head coach beats the hell out of being the son of another occupation when pursuing head coaching jobs. Number two is being a former professional player or highly successful college player. Great players don't always equate to being great coaches, but their pedigree usually affords them the opportunity. Third on the list is timing. The phrase "timing is everything" applies to most aspects of life, and college baseball is no exception. A head coach that retires, resigns, or God forbid dies on the job; opens the door for his assistant to slide into the vacated head coaching position. I, like many college baseball coaches, fall under category four, which is paying your dues. Those in category four often ask themselves, "How much shit am I willing to eat?" while chasing their dream. My roller coaster ride is entertaining, sometimes unbelievable, and an insightful behind-the-scenes look at the life of a college baseball coach.

I have had the privilege to build, or rebuild, four college baseball programs. These programs either did not exist or were on life support and were transformed into improbable winners. Many would accuse me of being a glutton for punishment, but the art of quickly transforming a despondent program into a winner is intrinsically rewarding and requires unwavering belief with a strong dose of steadfast determination. I wish I had a dollar for every time I've been told "you ought to write a book" by friends, fellow coaches, and acquaintances that hear my story for the very first time. My standard half-joking answer is, "nobody would believe it." The goal of *Cheers to Baseball* is to educate and inspire those in leadership positions that have been told they can't do something when facing long odds. While Baseball is the theme for the book, and the book contains plenty of baseball anecdotes; the message is valuable to coaches of other sports, administrators, business owners, and ALL aspiring leaders. Vince Lombardi, Hall of Fame football coach and five-time NFL champion, summed it up best, "The difference between a successful person and others is not a lack of strength, not a lack of knowledge, but rather is a lack of will."

I conceived many of the thoughts and ideas for my book in typical locations that folks do their best thinking...on the throne, in the shower, and staring through the windshield. Why *Cheers to Baseball* for a title? I firmly believe we all need a vehicle in life to assist in dictating our fate and provide a platform to best serve others. Baseball is my vehicle. Throughout the book, I toast Baseball and some of the many impactful people that I've been blessed to encounter, thanks to Baseball. I am hopeful *Cheers to Baseball* makes you laugh, provokes your thoughts, improves you as a leader, and motivates you to discover or enhance your vehicle in life.

# Chapter One:
# **No Outfield Fence**

Darren Munns
Assistant Baseball Coach
Drexel University
July 1991 – August 1998

I was bearing down on a Physical Education degree in the fall semester of my senior year when I realized I did not want to be a teacher. This is a helluva revelation when you have dropped thousands of dollars for your education, and the real world is looming in your near future. The phrase "pot committed" is poker terminology for a player reaching a point in a hand when folding their cards does not make sense. I was "pot committed" to becoming a teacher but desperately wanted to fold my cards. I attended Missouri Western State College to play college baseball, and school was an afterthought. I excelled at partying, poker, and pick-up basketball; yet, somehow I was getting eerily close to earning an undergraduate degree. My 84 mile per hour fastball was several ticks short on the radar gun for pro ball, so plan B was to become a college baseball coach. Student teaching during the upcoming spring semester was my final academic hurdle. No small feat, considering less than two-thirds of all college students earn a degree, and 30% of all college students drop out after their freshman year. In lieu of student teaching and responsible logic, I subscribed to the Eric Mason Plan.

Eric was one of the first people I met at Missouri Western, and we were definitely cut from the same cloth. He was a fast-talking hustler from Fort Smith, Arkansas and FUN was always his top priority. We spent more time at the dog track than in the library. The social aspect is what makes college exciting and enticing for those that choose to matriculate. However, at some point, a degree and joining the real world becomes a reality. A couple of famous movie lines illustrate the desire to stave off graduation and cherish every last bit of the college experience. Dean Wormer, the Dean of Students in *Animal House,* advised Kent "Flounder" Dorfman and his fraternity brothers, "Fat, drunk, and stupid is no way to go through life, son." An exchange from *Tommy Boy,* starring the late comedian Chris Farley, epitomizes the sloth-esque path many take on their journey through higher education.

Tommy: "Did you hear I graduated?"

Richard Hayden: "Yeah and just a shade under a decade too, all right."

Tommy: "You know a lot of people go to college for seven years."

Richard Hayden: "I know, they're called doctors."

Eric embodies the Contrarian Philosophy, which is taking the road less traveled. I find the Contrarian Philosophy to be sheer genius, as you will discover throughout the book. So what the hell is The Eric Mason Plan?

Eric aspired to coach college basketball, and also had

no desire to use his Physical Education degree to become a teacher. My partner in crime was smiling ear to ear, and talking a mile a minute. I would have predicted Eric had just hit a straight trifecta at the dog track, but instead, he had just returned from a meeting with his academic advisor. My Contrarian buddy had discovered two academic loopholes that became the Eric Mason Plan. Physical Education-General was a little-known undergraduate degree at Missouri Western that had never been achieved by a student. A student must complete all Physical Education requisites, but the student teaching component was not mandatory to obtain this "illustrious" degree. My mother, my academic advisor, and many other sane people asked, "Why in the hell would you get a PE degree if you can't teach?" A Missouri Western PE General degree isn't exactly an Ivy League accomplishment, but an undergraduate degree nonetheless. We were the charter members of the PE General club at Missouri Western. We soon became the only members of the club. After we walked across the graduation stage, the very next year the school's administration eliminated the PE General degree because they deemed it useless.

o o o o o o o o

There are special numbers that are synonymous with Baseball's history and fans. **4,256**: Pete Rose's all-time hits record. **755**: Hank Aaron's all-time home run record (sorry Barry Bonds, but this author still recognizes Aaron's 755). **56**: Joe DiMaggio's record hitting streak (even more impressive was Joe D marrying Marilyn Monroe), **2,632**: Cal Ripken Jr.'s consecutive games played record, **1.12**:

Bob Gibson's ERA for his iconic 1968 season. One of my favorite baseball questions that fans debate is, "What record will never be broken?" This one is easy. It is Cy Young's **511** wins. The game has changed dramatically as it applies to the starting pitcher. Complete games are a thing of the past, and in today's game, a starter is applauded if they contribute five innings to open a contest. Cy Young's 511 wins will never be sniffed by another hurler and you can book it! With all due respect to Charlie Hustle, The Hammer, The Yankee Clipper, The Iron Man, and Cy; let's take a deeper dive into Gibby's 1968 season. He made 34 starts and completed 28 of them with 13 shutouts. For context, during the 2019 season, Shane Bieber and Lucas Giolito led baseball with 3 complete games each. In the six starts, Gibson didn't complete in 1968, he was pinch hit for and was NEVER removed from the mound during an inning. Even more impressive was Major League Baseball adopting the "Gibson Rules" after the 1968 season. The mound was lowered from 15 inches to 10 inches, and the strike zone was lowered from a batter's armpits to the letters on his jersey. True greatness is when a person's actions alter the lives of those that come after them. Bob Gibson altered pitching after his 1968 season, and Eric Mason altered the PE General degree at Missouri Western! For the record, Eric never coached college basketball but is an extremely successful businessman. Nearly 30 years later we still raise our cocktail at Kansas City Chiefs tailgates to toast the PE General! Cheers to Baseball and Eric Mason!

Part two of the Eric Mason Plan that changed the course of my spring semester was the NCAA's one-time senior exception rule. Any senior satisfying graduation is allowed to take less than twelve credits in their final semester and is still eligible to participate in sports. I needed a three-credit PE internship to satisfy this newfound rule, so I coached a youth basketball team every Saturday morning in January to fulfill my internship requirement. My final semester of college had transitioned from a student teaching headache to playing baseball without having a single class. That, my friends, is truly jumping in a bucket of manure and coming out with a fresh haircut! Those four months were the only time in my life I've lived like a professional baseball player. Wake up for lunch, head to the ballpark, happy hour/dinner/ shenanigans, and repeat the process. My mother always said idle time gets you in trouble. However, the idle time I had during the spring semester helped land my first college coaching job.

Three teammates and I lived in a dilapidated two-story house our senior year. This ancient monstrosity was a true dump that became known as The Mansion. We strategically placed plastic buckets in the living room when it rained to solve a leaky roof. Due to extremely weak plumbing, pooping on the road was highly recommended. The plunger was an essential instrument at The Mansion. Despite these "features" you would never find in a real estate listing, rent was dirt cheap which provided more funds for happy hour. I was clueless about how to pursue a college baseball coaching job and sought the advice of my head coach, Doug Minnis. Coach Minnis was a throwback and graduated from the old school. He had a military background, was in his mid-60s and was a Hall of Fame character of the game. He chain-smoked Camel unfiltered cigarettes, continuously guzzled straight black coffee, and was never shy about delivering a profanity-laced ass chewing. The Coach Minnis stories are legendary amongst his former players. Coach Minnis advised I contact schools and inquire about assistant coaching positions. I departed his smoke-filled office smelling like a pack of Camels, but had a plan to become a college baseball coach. Cheers to Baseball and Coach Minnis, who recently passed away at 90 years young, and was a great influence to launch my coaching career.

The Mansion became my headquarters for an ongoing letter-a-thon. I mailed a letter to every NCAA Division 1 and NCAA Division 2 school in the country inquiring about an assistant coaching position, nearly 600 letters total. This was a monumental task banging away on an Apple Macintosh computer in 1991. I figured the odds were in my favor to land a job. 1/600 seemed like a lock! Reply letters from college head coaches nationwide were landing in The Mansion's mailbox. My excitement was building that I would be inundated with interview requests. I would soon realize that college coaching positions are coveted, and thus the Wall of Shame was created. After about the first 30 reply letters were rejections, my roommates decided to display them on a large wall in the dining room. A daily ritual had become my roommates fetching rejection letters from the mailbox, opening the letters while sitting around the poker table that served as our dining room table, busting my balls, and hanging the newly acquired rejection letters on the Wall of Shame. Cheers to Baseball and my room dogs DeWayne Hickey, Tommy Thies, and Jim Dapkus. Their ballbusting was priceless, "LSU Baby! Not a chance." "This team sucks and they still won't hire you!" "Munns, this guy doesn't even know how to spell your first OR last name." We hosted parties and informed guests that I was a prized high school football recruit, and these were letters from college coaches hopeful that I would be their next star quarterback. Much like directions when constructing your child's Christmas toy, it is amazing how many people don't read the fine print. Approximately half the schools actually replied to my letter, and there was ONE school that showed slight interest.

1991 was before the advent of cell phones. We had one cordless landline phone that was often lodged in a couch cushion, parked outside on the deck, or misplaced at an undisclosed location in The Mansion. "Munns, some guy from Drexler is on the phone!" Several attempts to lure me downstairs were made with this repeated message. Finally, the cordless phone was thrown into my upstairs bedroom. I was awoken from a drunken siesta when my impromptu phone interview began with Don Maines from Drexel (not Drexler) University. *Major League* is my favorite baseball movie. My "phone interview" with Coach Maines was reminiscent of the classic scene in *Major League* when Jake Taylor was drunk on a cot in Mexico, sprawled sideways, and wearing a sombrero when the phone rings. The call came from Cleveland Indians manager Lou Brown who asked the washed-up Taylor to play for the pitiful Indians. Taylor replied, "Is that you, Tolbert? This isn't very funny you know. I'm hungover and my knees are killing me and if you're gonna pull this shit at least you could have said you're from the Yankees." Don Maines was Lou Brown and Darren Munns was Jake Taylor. After a half-hour "phone interview" with Coach Maines I was planning a trip to Philly to pursue my first college coaching job at Drexel University.

I had just produced a pedestrian 4-3 season on the mound my senior year, and earned a PE General degree, but was now Philly-bound for my interview with Coach Maines. I had never been east of St. Louis, so needless to say this was a big deal. Conventional wisdom would be to purchase a round-trip flight and bear down on securing your first real job. In lieu of conventional wisdom, I convinced a couple of buddies to join me on an eight-day voyage to Philly while visiting seven Major League ballparks along the way. Tommy Thies, one of my room dogs, and my childhood/lifelong best buddy John Houf were on board for this excursion turned interview. The road from Missouri to Philly, and back, was littered with Major League stadiums. We studied the MLB schedule and mapped out one helluva trip in this geographical order: Chicago/Wrigley Field, Detroit/old Tiger Stadium, Cincinnati/Riverfront Stadium, Cleveland/Municipal Stadium (the Mistake by the Lake), Philly/Veterans Stadium, Baltimore/Memorial Stadium, and Chicago/Comiskey Park. A trip for the ages! We stayed with friends, former teammates, and Coach Maines put us up in a campus dorm for our two nights in Philly. All told, we only purchased one hotel room during our eight-day trip. In the midst of this glorious ballpark tour was my interview at Drexel.

Drexel University is located in downtown Philly, and it was culture shock for a kid from small town mid-Missouri. I didn't care because I had a shot to become a Division 1 baseball coach. Don Maines had completed one season as the skipper at Drexel when I interviewed. He took over the program late in the summer and had very little time to recruit for his first season. The Drexel Dragons finished 4-

34 in his first season and were the D1 version of the Bad News Bears. I'm confident you could recruit nine drunks from your local tavern and win four of 38 games! There have been statistically dreadful losers in every major sport. My favorite was the NFL's 1976 expansion Tampa Bay Buccaneers. The Bucs, rightfully nicknamed "the Yucs," were coached by quick-witted John McKay. 1976 brought a winless season of 0-14, and then they lost the first twelve games of 1977 to open the franchise with 26 consecutive losses. During this dubious losing streak, Coach McKay was asked about his team's execution. He replied, "I'm all for it." My interview with Coach Maines was wrapping up and he offered me the position to be his Pitching Coach for a whopping $1,000 annual salary. The most frugal tight ass couldn't make a grand last long in Philly. He also guaranteed me a job to work at the Princeton University Baseball Camp the three weeks before I started at Drexel. Coach Maines was an assistant coach at Princeton before he became the Drexel head coach. I would earn $900 in three weeks and stay at a dorm on Princeton's campus, while I figured out my housing in Philly. Many people would be insulted by his $1,900 proposition. I immediately accepted and couldn't wait to begin my coaching career. We shook hands and Coach Maines asked if I had any questions. At that moment, I realized I hadn't seen the baseball field. "Where do you guys play your games?" Don replied, "Oh, our field isn't great, but we can go have a look."

Drexel Field is the runaway winner for the worst ballpark in the history of college baseball. This plot of wasteland with a plate and three bases was located at 43$^{rd}$ and Powelton in the ghetto of West Philly and was a ten-minute drive from campus. My parents visited me once, and only once, during my seven years as a Philly resident. After touring Drexel Field, my Dad stated, "The best part about this shithole is seeing it in the rearview mirror." My road-tripping buddies and I followed Coach Maines through the projects before arriving at Drexel Field. As we approached from beyond right field, I asked, "Where's the outfield fence?" Coach Maines replied, "We don't have one." A Division 1 baseball program with no outfield fence! As we got closer to the infield it was apparent there were no dugouts. A couple of rundown wooden benches served as the "dugouts," with no overhead covering whatsoever. Our stroll finally led us to home plate. Only a six-foot chain-link fence separated the baseball facility and two high-rise housing project buildings. Drexel players referred to them as the twin towers, and they cast shadows on Drexel Field. *The Jeffersons* was a popular 1970s comedy sitcom that featured a family that had turned rags to riches and moved into a swank Manhattan high-rise apartment. The show's opening theme song, "Movin' on Up," was extremely popular with viewers and made them sing along at home. One line described the Jefferson's new digs as a "deee-luxe apartment in the sky!" Nothing was deluxe about the living accommodations in West Philly. Most Division 1 yards (baseball slang for ballpark) have netting that serves as the backstop behind home plate. The backstop, by rule, is located 60 feet behind home plate. Drexel Field had a chain-link backstop that barely left room for the catcher and umpire to perform their craft. The backstop's overhang was directly above the catcher's head. It was literally impossible to pop out to the catcher at Drexel Field, and challenging for the most fleet-of-foot base runner to advance a base on a wild pitch.

After our grand tour of this city park camouflaging as a Division 1 baseball facility, Coach Maines asked, "You still want the job?" I replied, "Absolutely!" After all, who wouldn't want to begin their adult life making $1,900 and calling Drexel Field home? Coach Maines ended our visit by proclaiming he liked Drexel Field because "once we recruit some good players it will be a helluva home field advantage." This Contrarian and ultra-competitive mindset epitomized Don Maines. We departed the parking lot at Drexel Field and I told Coach Maines I'd see him at Princeton. It was laughable that an assclown with a PE General degree would be residing at prestigious Princeton University in a few short months. Many thoughts raced through my mind during the long journey home. How would I pay my bills? Where would I live? How does a college baseball field not have an outfield fence? My brain was in overdrive like a base runner finding a new gear to stretch a double into a triple. The triple is one of the most exciting plays in baseball, and yet it has become nearly extinct in Major League Baseball. The career triples leader board is dominated by players from yesteryear. Sam Crawford is the all-time leader with 309. Baseball historians reason that older ballparks were more spacious which led to more triples. A valid point, but I believe a contributing factor to the triple decline is because players don't sprint from the batter's box. A triple is a 270 foot trip around the bases, but the difference between a double and a triple is determined by the hitter's effort level the first 30 feet out of the batter's box. Effort will take you a long way in baseball and in life!

I packed my small Plymouth Sundance to near

explosion with essential belongings. My second cross-country journey of the summer was underway. This journey was quite different than the eight-day joyride I took for my interview. I was taking the first step of my coaching career and it was a 1,000-mile trek to unknown territory. I called my Mom regularly while working at the Princeton camp. During a call, she told me I had a cousin living in Philadelphia, and I should look him up if I needed anything. Needed anything? I needed a place to live! Mark Jordan is my second cousin who I had only met a few times at family reunions. Mark grew up in Seattle and his work led him to Philly. We connected over the phone immediately and he invited me to stay with him until I found a place to live. Mark had a row house in suburban Philly. Row houses are, as the name suggests, connected brick homes lined up all in a row. This living arrangement is commonplace in Philly neighborhoods. Mark was working late the day I arrived so he left me a key to his house. My long lost cousin had taken me in, given me a key to his house, and hadn't seen me in years. The Beatles had a hit single in 1967, "With a Little Help from My Friends." I definitely got by with more than a little help from my friends during my time spent in Philly. Mark Jordan was the first of many to assist me in transitioning from small town USA to the City of Brotherly Love. Cheers to Baseball and Cousin Mark!

My biggest challenge during my initial days in Philly was figuring out where the hell I was going, and how in the hell I was going to get there. I felt like a one-legged duck swimming in a circle while learning to navigate the fourth largest city in the country. GPS did not exist in the early 90s. The "recalculating" alert from a computerized lady with a British accent was not an option for disoriented drivers. My pre-GPS strategies were to continue driving until I figured it out, pull into a gas station and ask for help, or motion for another car to roll down their window while at a stoplight and ask them for help. I left Cousin Mark's row house on a mission to purchase a case of beer and some food and stumbled upon a grocery store. My shopping was complete except for the case of beer. After wandering aimlessly around the store for a half-hour, I finally swallowed my pride and asked a worker where the liquor section was located. The worker smirked, "You not from around here?" He informed me that not only this grocery store didn't sell alcohol, but the state of Pennsylvania only sold alcohol in 'package stores.' I was perplexed by this disappointing discovery. Having rarely strayed from Missouri in my life, I was accustomed to purchasing alcohol in grocery stores, convenience stores, and gas stations. I finally found a package store to purchase my suds, and then I was on the road back to Cousin Mark's row house.

Then came an "oh shit" moment. I realized his address and his work phone number were on a slip of paper that I had left at his row house. How did we ever survive without cell phones?! Mark's neighborhood contained city block after city block of identical red brick row houses. The fact that they all looked exactly alike made finding his row house impossible. Thankfully I remembered the street name so I parallel parked my Plymouth Sundance, still packed with my life's belongings, and waited for a male figure to approach any of the row houses on the block. After all, I had not seen Cousin Mark in years and had no idea what he looked like. I enjoyed a few cold beers while curbside and asked several unsuspecting gentlemen if they were Mark Jordan. Eventually, the real Mark Jordan was found and I concluded my five-hour trip to the grocery store. This bumbling maiden voyage was a microcosm of my early days in Philly. I had a lot to learn to become a transplanted Philadelphian and had even more to learn about becoming a successful college recruiter.

Recruiting is relentless obsessive behavior that is the lifeblood for all winning programs. Even many diehard fans of college athletics don't realize the workload, and personal sacrifice, for a college recruiter. Recruiting is a 24/7 grind with no breaks. There is an old saying that it's the Johnnys and the Joes, not the Xs and the Os, that win games. You can't win the Kentucky Derby riding a jackass! Good players don't just show up on campus, especially at less than desirable programs. Drexel Baseball definitely qualified as less than desirable and had plenty of obstacles. Our lone selling point consisted of a letter and a digit; D 1! High school and junior college players are infatuated with the thought of playing Division 1 Baseball. Pete Rose once said, "I would walk through Hell in a gas suit to play baseball." Amateur players would march right behind Charlie Hustle for the chance to play D1 Baseball. I played the D1 card early and often with recruits, but a losing tradition was a major obstacle. Everybody loves a winner! The perception of Drexel Baseball among players, high school coaches, opposing college coaches, professional scouts, and anybody with a baseball pulse was either as an unknown commodity, or worse yet, the laughingstock of college baseball. Here are a few of my favorite comments that served as motivation to recruit my ass off:

"Where in the hell is Drexler?"

"If you win at Drexel, you can win any place in the country."

"I refuse to scout a game at Drexel Field because I value my safety."

"You guys ever get an outfield fence? That's the craziest shit I ever seen!"

"I didn't know Drexel had a baseball team."

Drexel University presented three major recruiting hurdles: facilities, academic curriculum, and expense. Drexel Field was a tough sell to recruits and their families, despite Coach Maines praising it as a home field advantage. What 18-year-old kid would find Drexel Field appealing? Drexel University is one of the leading engineering schools in the nation, but it did not offer a Physical Education degree (and certainly didn't offer a PE General). Unfortunately, very few good baseball players are Engineering majors, and many choose Physical Education as their major. Balancing the academic demands of pursuing an Engineering degree at a prestigious university, and the athletic demands of being a Division 1 baseball player are nearly impossible. Eric Moore was in our second recruiting class at Drexel, and was an exception to the rule. Big E graduated with honors, won 20 games on the mound, and had one helluva good time along the way. Eric and I remain close friends, and years after our coach/player relationship, we have enjoyed memorable times at Fenway Park, Busch Stadium, and Vegas. Cheers to Baseball and Eric Moore! Tuition was expensive, and the school only granted us roughly four baseball scholarships. The NCAA allows Division 1 baseball programs a maximum of 11.7 scholarships to construct a full roster of 25-35 players. I have no earthly idea why 11.7

is the chosen number that exists to this day. Maybe the original creator of this goofy number was an avid craps player. Each individual school determines how many scholarships are granted for their baseball program. Four scholarships presented a major challenge considering other schools in our league were fully funded. Ugly and broke is a bad combination! We were playing poker with fewer chips and lousy cards, but we were hell-bent on building Drexel baseball.

Don Maines was ultra-competitive and relished being an underdog. Coach Maines was a blue-collar grinder from North Jersey, and he had the uncanny ability to use "fuck" as a noun, verb, and adjective; often all in the same sentence. He was confident and determined to build Drexel Baseball against all odds. I learned invaluable lessons on how to build a college baseball program, which as you will find out, has benefited me throughout my career. I planned to stay one or two years at Drexel, but my stay turned into seven years thanks to my relationship with Coach Maines. I've been involved in college athletics for 35 years as a player or coach, and if I had to choose one coach to motivate a team before a game it would be Don Maines. Cheers to Baseball and Don Maines! Recruiting in its simplest form is identifying players, hosting players for campus visits, and signing players. Successful recruiters endure long road trips in search of players, make countless nightly phone calls to woo players, and in the end, are rejected by far more players than they sign. That final rejection call goes something like this, "Coach, I really want to thank you for all of your time and I really like you and your program, BUT..." Technology has made recruiting much easier. Many coaches today recruit from the comfort of their recliner. Livestream video, recruiting websites, social media, and many more touch-of-a-button conveniences are utilized by lazy recruiters. During my Drexel days recruiting required rigorous legwork to identify and eventually sign players. The early 90s was before cell phones, so I spent most evenings in the baseball office making recruiting calls while having a few cold ones. Many nights, after a four-hour call session, I had a logbook full of players that eventually signed with other programs, and a collection of empty beer cans for my efforts. The rejection-to-commitment ratio with recruits weighs heavily in favor of rejection. Recruiters suffer countless rejections before landing a verbal commitment. A verbal commitment from a talented player to attend Drexel was cause for celebration!

The figurative road to ultimately signing good players begins literally on the road itself. Most Division 1 athletic departments have a fleet of modern vehicles for their coaches to use for recruiting. Drexel Athletics had one beast of a vehicle in their "fleet," and it was a 1973 navy blue station wagon. This eyesore was known as the Dragon Wagon, and was so long it required two normal parking spots. *National Lampoon's Vacation* is a cinematic classic. The Dragon Wagon was the real-life Family Truckster. Clark W. Griswold would have felt right at home behind the wheel of the Dragon Wagon, with Aunt Edna's corpse strapped to the roof. I refuse to explain the movie reference; if you haven't seen *National Lampoon's Vacation* that's your own damn fault! Other coaches at Drexel chose to use their personal vehicle, and get reimbursed for mileage, instead of shamefully driving the Dragon Wagon. I claimed the Dragon Wagon all to myself and reserved it regularly. I spun the odometer all over the East Coast on our recruiting car that resembled a hearse. High school games, summer tournaments, and showcase camps were all frequent destinations while searching for future Drexel Dragons.

The recruiting trail for college coaches and professional scouts resembles a traveling carnival, as they all have the schedule of events so you consistently see the same group of recruiters. The college coaches are clones; 25-40-year-old men decked out in new running shoes or casual loafers, khaki shorts or khaki pants, polo shirts emblazoned with their school logo, and either a baseball cap or bucket hat also displaying their school logo. The professional scouts are easy to pinpoint during the dog days of summer because they are required to wear long pants. Why Major League Baseball organizations enforce this pointless policy is beyond me. If I owned an MLB franchise, I could care less if a scout wore nothing but a jockstrap if he had a keen eye for talent. At popular recruiting events/games, coaches and scouts jostle for position behind home plate to gain the best possible vantage point to evaluate players. All evaluators are equipped with the tools of the trade; a stopwatch and radar gun. The stopwatch is primarily used to time a hitter's foot speed from the batter's box to first base (home to first in baseball lingo), and to time how quickly a catcher delivers his throw to second base on a stolen base attempt (pop time in baseball lingo). The radar gun measures the velocity of pitches in miles per hour (velo in baseball lingo). "What's his velo?" is the most popular question uttered in baseball circles. Recruiters demonstrate a wide range of attention spans while working at their craft.

There are three types of recruiters. Type one takes copious notes on every single player. Type two watches attentively and only jots notes when a player catches their fancy. Type three just enjoys looking the part and bullshits with another coach who also enjoys looking the part. Type three doesn't realize that recruiting equals winning. They probably won't last long in the profession and will bitch about getting their ass kicked because they have bad players. I recruited like a madman because you have no choice when you are 4-34.

I was no different than many young and underpaid aspiring college baseball coaches that make personal sacrifices for an opportunity to get their foot in the door. How do you get experience without a job? How do you get a job without experience? These two questions represent a dizzy dilemma, for those seeking their first job, in most occupations. In the college baseball world, your first job is usually a volunteer or part-time opportunity to start your career. The biggest sacrifice I made was sleep. I prescribed to Babe Ruth's theory that you can sleep when you're dead. George Herman "Babe" Ruth is a larger-than-life figure that, for my money, is the greatest baseball player that ever walked the planet. He had the coolest nicknames; The Babe, The Bambino, The Sultan of Swat, and old Yankee Stadium was even coined "The House that Ruth Built." In 1920, he hit 54 home runs, which were more home runs than EVERY other TEAM in baseball. 'Who is the greatest baseball player of all time?' always conjures debate amongst baseball fans. Arguments are made for Willie Mays, Hank Aaron, Mickey Mantle, Stan Musial, Ted Williams, Barry Bonds, Mike Trout (someday), and other baseball legends. Babe Ruth sported a 94-46 record as a pitcher before he became a full-time hitter. His dominance on the mound and at the plate makes him my runaway choice.

I held an array of jobs that paid my rent at various humble abodes. After my temporary stay with Cousin Mark, I shared my first apartment with fellow Drexel assistant coach, John Szefc. My move to the inner city introduced me to the Philadelphia Parking Authority, which became my constant nemesis. This militant and money-hungry nuisance, known as the PPA, always seized the opportunity to administer a parking ticket. They cut motorists ZERO slack. The meter maids in Philly earned such a pain-in-the-ass reputation they prompted A&E Network to feature them on the reality TV show, *Parking Wars*. Needless to say, Munns vs. the PPA was an ongoing battle. John and I resided in a three-room rat trap above a pizza shop near Drexel's campus. Turning the lights on before entering this closet of an apartment was highly recommended to give the mice a chance to scurry under the appliances. Coach Szefc's surname resembles an eye chart used to test your vision during a visit to the optometrist, but nothing was confusing about his baseball acumen. John has climbed the Division 1 coaching ladder and is currently the Head Baseball Coach at Virginia Tech University. We still laugh about our days drinking Old Milwaukee tall boys, watching our twelve-inch TV, and talking baseball. Coach Szefc was serving as the Assistant Coach at Kansas State University when they visited Columbia, MO for a weekend series vs. Mizzou. He spent one of his evenings having dinner and drinks at the Munns' residence in Columbia. The sign of a true friendship is resuming conversation, and sharing laughs, without missing a beat when you see each other infrequently. We sat in my basement and picked up right where we left off; sharing memories, talking baseball, and laughing the night away. I had flashbacks to our days dodging mice in Philly when we had similar evenings. Cheers to Baseball and John Szefc!

More complex than finding a place to live, was finding a flexible second job that allowed me to perform my duty as a full-time college baseball coach. I was a doorman at a bar, worked nights loading airplanes at UPS, taught pitching lessons to high school players, and eventually became a chauffeur to pay my bills. Imagine that, after two years in Philly, a lost soul that could not get to the grocery store and back, was now a chauffeur! I worked five years as a chauffeur for a black car service that catered to corporate America. The company was extremely accommodating, and I could create my own work schedule around Drexel Baseball. Most days my shift was very early in the morning until the early afternoon. I had learned to navigate Philly, and the surrounding area, thanks to my many recruiting trips. The job's greatest challenges were the 3 AM start times and wearing a suit and necktie. Nothing like strapping a tie around my sleep-deprived neck at 3 AM to be a college baseball coach! I had rarely worn a tie in my life, and when I did it was a clip-on tie. During my first season at Drexel, we took a team flight to Boston for a conference weekend series vs. Northeastern University. Players and coaches were in a single file line and walking through the metal detector chamber at Logan Airport. I proceeded to take my turn and the metal detector began beeping. I pulled my slacks pockets inside out and assured airport security I did not have anything in my pockets. I backed up, repeated the process, and the metal detector went off again. At this point, a security officer used his hand-held wand to scan me head-to-toe. His wand was activated under my chin and he asked if I was wearing jewelry or military dog tags. A light went off in my head and I realized it was my clip-on necktie that was the problem. I unclipped my tie and dropped it in the security container as the players behind me laughed hysterically. Ted Williams once said, "You don't have to wear a necktie, if you hit .400." I never hit .400 so I kept strapping on my necktie at 3 AM!

I was fueled by Diet Pepsi, Redman chewing tobacco, and No Doz caffeine tablets during my limo driving days. My first run was almost always picking up a client in the Philly suburbs, and chauffeuring them to Philadelphia International Airport (PIA) to catch the first flight out of town. There were a plethora of name-brand hotels in close proximity to PIA. I used my breaks between runs to grab some shuteye in the back of the limo, while stationed in the parking lot of the Hilton, Embassy Suites, Marriott, or any number of five-star hotels. Luxury hotels provide delicious breakfasts and clean restrooms. I picked my palace on hotel row, confidently strolled into their lobby, grabbed a complimentary USA Today newspaper, and filled my plate full of vittles. My coat-and-tie attire, poker face, and "kill 'em with kindness" approach allowed me to enjoy many complimentary breakfasts as a "guest of the hotel." I always left a gratuity for the staff. People that have been in the service business, and have relied on tips, understand this kind gesture. Coach Maines taught this life lesson during overnight road trips. Each Drexel player was required to leave a minimum one dollar tip for the cleaning staff on departure day. The hotel lobby restroom secures my top ranking as the most desirable location for a "road deuce." All travelers have been faced with locating a restroom when their bowels are ready to move. The hotel lobby restroom has all the essential attributes for a quality experience; cleanliness, two-ply toilet paper (nothing worse than muddy knuckles), the privacy of one throne, and they are air-conditioned to a cool temperature during the summer months. This tip alone makes reading my book worthwhile. Nothing worse than sweating while taking a dump!

My sleep deprivation was part job related, and part self-induced, from late-night trips to Atlantic City (commonly known as AC to Philly and Jersey natives). The Atlantic City Expressway is a 44-mile stretch of straight highway that connects Philly and AC. This approximate one-hour door-to-door venture from my residence to a casino blackjack table was both a blessing and a curse. I was an avid poker player throughout my upbringing, and a big fan of gambling in general. Coaching buddies, colleagues, and friends from all walks of life comprised my inner circle of gambling buddies. Impromptu AC runs were commonplace, and the instigator usually didn't have to ask twice. Las Vegas continuously builds new shiny gambling castles because the majority of gamblers lack the two most important traits for success; they are uneducated regarding the strategies and nuances of their game of choice, and they are undisciplined with their bankroll. Kenny Rogers's classic song, *The Gambler,* simplistically explains this principle with this famous lyric, "you got to know when to hold 'em, know when to fold 'em, know when to walk away, and know when to run..."

My vast poker experience and feel for gambling gave me a chance to compete in the casino. My blessing was hitting a big lick (gambling term for winning a large amount of money), which allowed me to drive the limo less and spend more time being a college baseball coach. My curse was taking a bath (gambling term for losing your ass), which meant more time behind the wheel to make up for lost dough. A gambler that says he's never taken a bath is like a pitcher saying he's never had a rough outing: THEY ARE LYING! Casinos are kind enough to give you a complimentary room or meal if your gambling session is lengthy (known as comps to casino personnel and gamblers). The "comp" meal makes a gambler feel important, but in actuality, it's merely a parting gift for their donation.

The limo gig was necessary to supplement my income, and I could write a separate book about my career as a chauffeur. My all-time favorite story came after an all-nighter in AC. I was dispatched to the Philly suburbs in the early morning hours to transport a gentleman to John F. Kennedy Airport (JFK) in New York City. I regularly made the trip to JFK, and if traffic cooperated this was a two to three-hour journey. I staged the brand new Lincoln Town Car in the driveway of my client's residence, seated groggily behind the wheel, while waiting for him to emerge from his mansion. He bounced out of his front door full of energy, and I greeted him with an enthusiastic smile and firm handshake. I had become an expert at flipping the switch from zombie to professional driver during these pre-dawn runs. As I loaded his suitcases in the trunk, my client slowly walked around the vehicle like an interested customer at an auto dealership. He asked how I liked the Lincoln Town Car, and informed me he was considering purchasing one for himself. I replied that it was a smooth ride, and half-jokingly said he could take it for a "test drive" to JFK this morning. His eyes lit up like a hitter identifying a belt-high fastball, and he accepted my offer. Sworn to secrecy, and role reversal in place, my client chauffeured Yours Truly to New York City while I drooled into a deep sleep in the back seat. We safely arrived at JFK, he thanked me for the opportunity, and tipped me a hundred bucks. Not a bad tip for taking a three-hour nap!

o o o o o o o

The recruiting efforts were getting better results on the field, which made my personal sacrifices seem worthwhile. Coach Maines' first recruiting class was instrumental in improving the program from 4-34 to 19-26. The 15-win turnaround was the largest in Division 1 Baseball. The following season we improved to 24-24 and lost in the championship game of our conference tournament to the University of Maine. In two years Drexel Baseball had gone from a 4-34 laughingstock to within one game of qualifying for an NCAA Regional berth. The program had been built with tough, hard-nosed kids primarily from Philly and the surrounding area. People in the college baseball world were starting to take notice, and a Drexel Baseball alum also took notice. I was sitting in the baseball office making nightly recruiting calls when an older gentleman barged in the office looking for the baseball coach. I introduced myself as the assistant coach and struck up a conversation. He informed me he was a former

Drexel player and wanted to help out the baseball program because he was impressed with the program's newfound success. That chance encounter led to subsequent conversations between John McElgin, who owned a successful engineering business, and Coach Maines. John eventually donated his services to build dugouts, replace the city backstop with state-of-the-art netting, and construct an outfield fence at Drexel Field. An insightful lesson I learned from Coach Maines is you never know who you are talking to when you meet a stranger, and that was certainly the case with John McElgin. Drexel Field was not the crown jewel of college baseball, but we had an outfield fence! That home field advantage Coach Maines predicted was coming to fruition.

Opposing teams dreaded traveling to the West Philly projects to play at Drexel Field. The University of Maine Black Bears was a powerhouse in the late 80s and early 90s, having appeared in the College World Series in Omaha multiple times. Due to conferences being realigned, Maine was making their inaugural visit to Drexel Field. We were in the midst of pre-game batting practice (universally known in baseball as BP) when I spotted the Black Bears' customized charter bus entering the parking lot of the high-rise projects, instead of parking in the appropriate lot located adjacent to the field. Coach Maines instructed me to "wait until they completely unload their fancy fucking bus and then tell them where to park." This was an ingenious way to welcome our guests! Orono, Maine is home to the Black Bears and is the absolute antithesis of West Philly. As I approached their completely unloaded bus, their assistant coach asked, "OK if we park in the dorm parking lot?" I replied, "Those aren't dorms Brother, those are the projects!" He looked like he had seen a ghost and they hurriedly loaded their bus while being verbally abused by the tenement residents. They hightailed it to the proper parking lot and unloaded their bus a second time. We won the game 1-0 and it was a milestone win that helped launch a new era of Drexel Baseball. The mighty Black Bears had been shocked by Drexel Field!

Towson State was a solid program in our league and was visiting Drexel Field for a conference game. During the middle of the contest, and with Drexel trailing, a round of gunfire rattled loudly in the projects. Umpires, coaches, and players (especially the Towson players) instantly halted play; and a buzz filtered through the spectators wondering what the hell just happened. All heads were on a swivel debating if they had heard gunfire or fireworks. Games had been delayed due to adolescent children and bums wandering onto the field, but never gunfire! The home plate umpire walked toward the exit and yelled at Coach Maines, "I'm outta here Donnie, and you will never see me ump a game here again! You can keep the check!" Play resumed with one umpire, and we came from behind to win on a bases loaded balk in the bottom of the ninth inning. Drexel Field had shocked, and in this case, shell shocked, another opponent.

Lehigh University visited Drexel Field to play a mid-week game. Lehigh is located in Bethlehem, PA approximately an hour and a half northwest of Philly. Opposing coaches typically spend part of the pre-game BP exchanging pleasantries, and shooting the breeze about all things baseball-related. Lehigh's Head Coach at the time was a young lad that probably had yet to celebrate his 30th birthday. He appeared more like a baby-faced freshman player than the skipper of a Division 1 baseball program. He spent the majority of our pre-game BP chat gazing wide-eyed at the surrounding area, and rambling about how his players spent the entire bus ride to Philly complaining about Drexel Field. Lehigh's "fearless" leader, and his troops, were defeated before the umpire ever yelled "play ball." Our home dugout was located on the first base side of the field, and the visitor's hut was positioned on the third base side. Early in the game, while Lehigh was in the field playing defense and we were batting, a loud ruckus broke out in the Lehigh dugout. The dugout had roughly a two-inch gap of open space between its' back wall and concrete floor. Some neighborhood kids preyed on Lehigh's dugout like they were shoplifting at a local sporting goods store, and were blindly reaching under the dugout wall fishing for baseball gear. Coach Maines sprinted from his post in the third base coaching box, and stomped on an unsuspecting juvenile's hand which was clutching a baseball bat. Coach Maines saved the bat, and further theft, with his swift actions. The kids scurried from the scene while exchanging expletives with Coach Maines. Lehigh coaches and players were aghast after having a front-row seat for this larceny. Lehigh Baseball was minus a few gloves and bats, a West Philly youth had a sore hand, and we proceeded to kick the shit out of our guests from Bethlehem!

These hard-to-believe stories illustrate why recruiting was an endless endeavor, requiring thorough homework, to sign players that possessed the toughness and talent to build Drexel Baseball. However, recruiting is the ultimate inexact science, and don't let anybody tell you differently.

We had a partial scholarship left to sign one more player to complete my first recruiting class. Coach Maines received a lead from an old coaching buddy about an undersized kid in Toronto named Kris Doiron. I made an initial phone call to Kris, and followed up with a call to his high school coach for a background check. After several failed transfers and disconnections by the high school secretary, a random high school guidance counselor landed on the receiving end of my call. Frustrated with the disconnections, and tired of searching for the baseball coach, I introduced myself and asked the unsuspecting counselor what he could tell me about Kris Doiron. Obviously, he missed the detail that I coached baseball and not hockey. "Kris is the best hockey player in the province. He'd be in the NHL if he was six inches taller." I reaffirmed that I coached baseball and he nonchalantly stated, "he's pretty good at baseball too." Kris flew into PIA for his recruiting visit and I met him at his gate. His visit was long before the 9/11 terrorist attacks, and airports still allowed gate pickups. I stationed myself at Kris' gate and waited patiently displaying a sign bearing his name, much like I had done thousands of times while picking up clients as a limo driver. Several athletic-looking young men deboarded the plane but walked right past me and my sign. As the passengers were thinning out, and the plane was nearly empty, I thought Kris Doiron had missed his flight. Then a young Canadian gentleman measuring 5'6" and a biscuit shy of 180 pounds sauntered toward me wearing casual loafers, cargo shorts, a plain white t-shirt, topped off with a Budweiser bucket hat. I smiled and welcomed Kris to Philly. In my mind, I thought "Holy shit! There's no way this guy can play!"

I learned a valuable lesson: Baseball players, unlike most sports, produce great players of all shapes and sizes. We decided to roll the dice and sign the diminutive Canadian we had never seen play, and as they say, "the rest is history." Kris was the final piece of a loaded recruiting class that propelled Drexel Baseball into a perennial conference contender, and highly regarded mid-major program. The cat that I originally met in the Budweiser bucket hat had balls like a burglar. He finished his Drexel career with 26 wins on the mound, locked down the three-hole in our lineup for four seasons, finished with a .370 career batting average, and owns almost every record in the history of Drexel Baseball. His most remarkable feat was rarely striking out as a hitter. He led the nation in the fewest strikeouts per at bats for two of his four seasons and finished his career with only thirteen strikeouts in 801 plate appearances. Kris was tagged with the nickname "Frenchy" during his freshman year by teammate Felix Donato, and boy did it stick. An athlete, or artist, truly has achieved legendary status when they are recognized by one name. Lawrence Peter Berra was one of the greatest catchers in baseball history, but he is known as Yogi in baseball lore. You see the name Elvis, and your first thought is not Elvis Aaron Presley, but the King of Rock n' Roll. Ichiro Suzuki had "Ichiro" stitched on the back of his Mariners jersey, instead of Suzuki, because he was a one-name sensation. Many baseball fans would not know Suzuki was his surname if they were surveyed. Almost 30 years later, I cross paths with coaches and opposing players from my Drexel days, and they still ask me about "Frenchy." Cheers to Baseball and Frenchy!

Roy Hallenbeck is a dear friend, and was a fellow

assistant coach at Drexel for three seasons. We shared a condo in South Jersey and our hobbies were drinking beer, watching baseball, and talking baseball until the wee hours of most mornings (sounds like a common theme with my roommates). Coach H is one of the best hitting coaches I've encountered, but was engaged to be married and had to forego his part-time Drexel coaching position to pursue a "real job." He was hired as Physical Education teacher and Head Baseball Coach at Millville High School in Millville, NJ. Coach H inherited a youngster named Mike Trout, and had the privilege of being his high school baseball coach. Yes, THAT Mike Trout! To this day, Coach H claims Mike Trout is the second best hitter he ever coached.......behind Frenchy! Not bad for a blind date from Toronto that "was pretty good at baseball too." Cheers to Baseball and Coach H!

Drexel Baseball was transformed from a 4-34 mess into a legitimate Division 1 baseball program. We shattered season win totals, appeared in three conference championship games, and graduated over 90% of our players. Most importantly, a prideful winning tradition was instilled at a place where a prideful winning tradition had been previously unimaginable. Administration can make or break an athletic department, or athletic program. I have been bamboozled throughout my career that athletic administrators are hired despite having no experience as a coach, or even worse, no athletic background whatsoever. I would never expect to be hired as the Department Chair for a college biology department, since I barely achieved a passing grade in Biology, yet non-athletic people are frequently chosen to lead athletic departments. Our on-field success, and serving as model ambassadors for Drexel University, did not prevent new athletic administration to reduce our already pathetic scholarship budget; a clear indication that baseball was not important to the current regime. We were also transitioning into the Colonial Athletic Association, which was a much stronger baseball conference than the America East. This recipe for failure, and my seven years of burning the candle at both ends, had finally gotten the best of me. I threw in the towel and resigned as the assistant baseball coach at Drexel. Unfortunately, my instincts were correct and Drexel University dropped their baseball program four years after my resignation. During my tenure, I turned down coaching jobs at more prestigious schools, and scouting opportunities in professional baseball, but have no regrets about remaining loyal to Drexel Baseball. A framed picture of my Drexel uniform, that I was gifted upon my departure, still hangs in my man cave today.

A future chapter in the book is dedicated to the importance of having fun, and I certainly had fun in Philly. I took full advantage of attending a multitude of live sporting events, concerts, and lived life to the fullest during my Philly experience. Here are my top ten highlights in descending order that I had the pleasure to attend:

10) Numerous championship boxing matches in Atlantic City. The atmosphere and adrenaline of a prizefight is an absolute thrill.

9) Concerts headlined by some of the top artists of all-time. A few favorites included Guns n' Roses, Garth Brooks, Nirvana, Jimmy Buffett, and the Rolling Stones.

8) Charles Barkley's return to Philly as a Phoenix Sun. Sir Charles is a personal favorite and one of the great personalities in the history of sports.

7) Major League Baseball All-Star Games hosted at Camden Yards (Baltimore 1993), Three Rivers Stadium (Pittsburgh 1994), and Veterans Stadium (Philly 1996). All the stars in one location were worth the price of admission.

6) Padres-Yankees World Series, game one, 1998 at old Yankee Stadium. Being in the presence of history at fabled Yankee Stadium gave me goosebumps. Seeing Tony Gwynn homer, Derek Jeter play shortstop, and Mariano Rivera pitch in the World Series was priceless.

5) Blue Jays-Phillies World Series, game four, 1993 at Veterans Stadium. This 15-14 classic slugfest is the highest-scoring World Series game in history.

4) The Palestra for many college basketball games. The "Cathedral for College Basketball" is a bucket list item for all college hoops fans.

3) Philadelphia Eagles games at Veterans Stadium with a sideline pass. An NFL game at field level is faster than I ever imagined!

2) Army-Navy games at Veterans Stadium. The pageantry of the Cadets and Midshipmen marching into the stadium is better than the game itself.

1) Duke-Kentucky NCAA Mid-Atlantic Regional tournament game at The Spectrum. The "Christian Laettner Game" is arguably the greatest college basketball game of all time, and exemplifies March Madness. One million people will say they were in

attendance, but I have a ticket stub to prove I was in the house when Laettner beat the buzzer.

My car was pointed west and I was Missouri bound. I was at a crossroads not only in my career, but in my life. Logical young adults with a college degree would feel frustrated being unemployed, homeless, and broke as they exited their 20s. My Contrarian outlook on life was quite the opposite. I cherished my Philly Experience, and departed with great memories, lifelong friendships, and a stack of unpaid parking tickets (they have since been paid). The Philadelphia Parking Authority can kiss my ass! Most importantly, I had received a top notch education from Don Maines on how to build a college baseball program against all odds.

# Chapter Two:
# BP with Jeff

Darren Munns
Head Baseball Coach
Harris-Stowe State University
September 2003 – September 2005

I completed the seventeen-hour power trip from Philly and pulled into my parents' driveway in Mexico, MO, with an uncertain future to say the least. Seven years previous I sat in the exact same driveway, before departing for Philly, with a future equally as uncertain. Not exactly progress! A mother is usually less than excited that her 29-year-old son is unemployed and returning to the nest, but my Mom was ecstatic. She had attributed every gray hair in her head to my time spent in Philly. The return home purposely corresponded with my favorite holiday, Thanksgiving Eve. Unlike New Year's Eve, which resembles Amateur Night for irresponsible partying, Thanksgiving Eve is a genuine reunion of old friends. The perfect Thanksgiving Eve consists of congregating in your hometown watering hole, while sharing memorable stories of yesteryear, and laughing your ass off. This particular Thanksgiving Eve was true to form, but also landed me an escape plan from living with Mom and Dad. I love my parents dearly, but pride alone should motivate a grown ass man to vacate his boyhood bedroom. Besides, family is like prime tequila; a couple shots are good for the soul, but more than that will make you sick! The local tavern was packed, and I was bouncing from one conversation to the next, catching up on lost time with my hometown comrades. I discovered that an old buddy was renting an apartment in nearby Columbia, MO, and was in dire need of a roommate. We shook hands, toasted our beers, and I instantly paid him in cash for my first month's rent while standing at the bar. Cheers to Baseball and Pat Talbott!

I contracted a severe case of positive culture shock upon my return to mid-Missouri. The Midwest's redeeming qualities had been taken for granted during my hiatus to the East Coast. First and foremost was the cost of living. My final two months in Philly I worked 70-hour weeks driving the limo to ease the financial burden of soon being jobless in Missouri. My bankroll also benefited from hitting a big lick in Atlantic City on my way out of town. A well-timed last hurrah in AC! By my humble standards, I was enjoying a lavish mid-Missouri existence while in relax mode. My break from the big-city bustle was therapeutic and allowed me peace of mind from the rigors of recruiting. Doctors that are on-call around the clock never shut off their mind, and must be prepared to act on a moment's notice. Obviously, a recruiter's job description pales in comparison to curing the sick and saving lives, but is similar in principle. Hall of Fame NFL coach Dick Vermeil first popularized the phrase 'coaching burnout,' and cited this self-inflicted condition as the reason he retired in 1983, only two years removed from a Super Bowl appearance with the Philadelphia Eagles. Coach Vermeil was known for working twenty-hour days, sleeping in his office, and repeating the process. I was not suffering from "coaching burnout," but a variation incurred by college coaches that I term "recruiting burnout." I weaned my brain from recruiting overdrive during the initial post-Drexel days, and used the quiet time to plot my next move....to Vegas!

I had ample time, especially without a J O B, to plan my next leap of faith to Sin City. The preliminary details of my grandiose brainstorm were to roll into Vegas in January, find living quarters and a job (limo gigs are plentiful in Vegas), and test my poker skills vs. the best players in the world. Despite a successful run at Drexel, college coaching jobs were a near impossibility due to the cut throat nature of the profession. I was prepared to pursue my other passion. Jim Dapkus, one of my college roomies from the Mansion, was the Head Baseball Coach at Central Methodist University (CMU), located in tiny Fayette, MO, a half-hour from Columbia. Coach Dapkus persuaded me to help coach his players during voluntary off-season workouts in December. My random trip to CMU would quickly become a life-changing event. Small-college coaches are usually glorified Admissions Counselors that work directly with their Admissions Department in the recruitment of student-athletes. Each athletic team is required to fill an oversized roster quota that financially behooves the school. My first day on campus I was sitting in Coach Dapkus' office discussing practice plans when a female Admissions Counselor popped in for a recruiting update. That fateful day I met my soul mate, best friend and love of my life. The Vegas plan was canceled! We celebrated our 20th wedding anniversary New Year's Eve of 2020. The second best tip I reveal in this book, other than the "road deuce," is to get married, remarried, or renew your wedding vowels on New Year's Eve. I realize that I previously criticized New Year's Eve / Amateur Night; all the more reason to provide family and friends a meaningful self-contained celebration to usher in the New Year. Cheers to Baseball and Sarah Munns! Cheers to Baseball and Sarah Munns! That's not a typographical error, because of her unwavering tolerance and faith as my First Lady, she is the only toast in the book that is worthy of a double!

The random off-season workouts at CMU turned into a volunteer coaching position for two seasons. My volunteer job description was to assist with practices and games but assume zero recruiting responsibility. This was an ideal formula to combat "recruiting burnout." CMU provided lasting friendships, and we achieved winning seasons on the field including a conference championship game appearance. My leftover Philly bankroll was nearing the end, and marriage requires a real job. I reluctantly quit as the volunteer coach at CMU, and the next two years were the only time in my life I was not a college baseball coach. It was an odd feeling not wearing baseball pajamas (baseball terminology for uniform) during the spring. Why is baseball the only sport that the coaches wear uniforms? Can you imagine Mike Krzyzewski in shorts and a tank top coaching Duke Basketball? How about Nick Saban prowling the Alabama sideline in football gear? Baseball historians offer no good reason for this long-standing custom. Connie Mack managed in a suit and tie at the turn of the 20th century, but formal game attire was phased out and replaced with managers and coaches wearing baseball pajamas. The National Past Time has featured "lifers" pulling on their baseball pajamas deep into senior citizenship. Don Zimmer, a.k.a. Zim or Popeye, was in uniform as a player, coach, and manager for 65 years. Red Schoendienst spent 74 consecutive seasons wearing baseball pajamas during his Hall of Fame career, including 67 seasons with the St. Louis Cardinals. "The Old Redhead," as long-time Cardinals broadcaster Mike Shannon refers to him, last wore the Birds on the Bats iconic Cardinals uniform at the ripe age of 95! Jimmie Reese coached into his early 90s with the Angels and was a true legend of the game. A fungo bat is a thin bat used to hit ground balls and fly balls so players can practice their defensive craft. Reese earned the reputation as the game's best fungo hitter, amazing players with his ability to place baseballs wherever he wanted with his magic wand. He was even known to use his fungo bat to "throw" batting practice. Jimmie Reese was Babe Ruth's roommate, and Nolan Ryan respected him so much that he named his son Reese. These three baseball gems illustrate the special privilege of wearing baseball pajamas!

A close friend and fellow Contrarian, Doc Moore, was opening an airport shuttle business in Columbia that transported passengers to the St. Louis and Kansas City airports. The shuttles departed every hour from Columbia to STL and KC, starting at 5 AM, and there were return shuttles every hour transporting passengers back to Columbia, which is centrally located in the Show Me State (90 minutes west of St. Louis and 90 minutes east of Kansas City). I was the first driver Doc hired to launch his shuttle business. Don Maines taught me how to build a college baseball program against all odds, and I was literally along for the ride to witness Doc Moore transform a start-up operation into a prosperous regional transportation giant. He ran an existing airport shuttle company out of business, doubled his van fleet, and added charter buses with terminals in Missouri and Illinois. Life often provides lessons from unsuspecting sources that are indirectly relative to your area of expertise. Doc Moore was to transportation what Don Maines was to college baseball; beating the odds by forming a fearless plan, executed with a tireless work ethic, and an undeniable will. Cheers to Baseball and Doc Moore! My favorite success story against all odds also involved the transportation industry. Yale undergraduate student, Fred Smith, submitted a paper for his Economics class outlining an overnight delivery service. The professor issued Fred a C for his efforts, and his "average" idea later blossomed into worldwide leader FedEx. Fred turned a C paper into billions, that's **billions** with a **B**! Mr. Smith is an ambitious genius and his Economics professor is an oblivious dumbass that should have been teaching basic PE courses at Missouri Western. I was tired of driving a van for a living, had the itch to wear baseball pajamas again, and was in high pursuit of becoming a Head Baseball Coach.

Although hard to explain to a layman, coaching is naturally in some people's blood. Dick Vermeil's "coaching burnout" subsided, and he came out of retirement as a successful broadcaster, to coach again. Coach Vermeil led the St. Louis Rams to a Super Bowl title in 1999, and later resurrected the Kansas City Chiefs into a playoff contender (2001-2005). College coaching websites feature available jobs at all levels of collegiate athletics. I religiously scanned the websites and applied to schools throughout the country that listed open baseball positions, and I was religiously rejected. Email rejection had replaced snail mail rejection, but this was the Wall of Shame sequel! There is an old adage for college baseball coaches that rings true, "Once you get out, it's hard to get back in." I had delivered a shuttle van of passengers to St. Louis' Lambert International Airport and was reading the St. Louis Post-Dispatch sports page when I read a blurb that Harris-Stowe State's baseball coach had resigned. Harris-Stowe is a historically black college located in inner city St. Louis and is a member of the NAIA (National Association of Intercollegiate Athletics). The NAIA is a separate organization from the NCAA and carries the stigma of being less prestigious than the NCAA. I had vaguely heard of the Harris-Stowe Hornets and followed up because desperate times call for desperate measures. I called the main number for the Athletic Department and an angel answered my call. Valerie Beeson, respectfully known as Ms. Beeson, had served Harris-Stowe in various capacities for 30+ years, was semi-retired, and was a consultant for the school. I later discovered she worked for the NAIA national office, was in the NAIA Hall of Fame, and was a walking rule book for the NAIA. More impressive, she mentored Harris-Stowe student-athletes and poured her heart and soul into positively impacting droves of young people. I had a pleasant 15-minute chat/phone interview with Ms. Beeson, she took my number, and guaranteed the Athletic Director would call me soon. Cheers to Baseball and Valerie Beeson!

Rich Fanning had served one month as the Harris-Stowe Athletics Director and his first task was hiring a baseball coach. As Ms. Beeson promised, Rich called the next day and asked if I would be interested in interviewing for the position. Faced with the prospect of driving a van for the rest of my life, I quickly accepted his request. Rich is an avid sports buff like myself, and my interview replicated a couple of old friends laughing and talking sports for three hours. The position was part-time and paid $5,000. Rich offered me the position on the spot, and I accepted the position on the spot. I finally was a college Head Baseball Coach! Cheers to Baseball and Rich Fanning! My wife had a great job in Columbia, so relocating was not an option. The challenge was living in Columbia and working a real job with benefits, while simultaneously being the CEO of a college baseball program two hours away in St. Louis. I concocted a master plan to mesh both of my occupations. Doc Moore agreed for me to drive the 5 AM shuttle to the St. Louis Airport, layover in St. Louis, and drive the 8 PM shuttle back to Columbia. Harris-Stowe was only 15 minutes from the airport, so this worked perfectly to perform both jobs. My daily chaotic schedule was as follows:

Depart Columbia at 5 AM and deliver a Mo-X shuttle van of passengers to the St. Louis Airport / Arrive at Harris-Stowe mid-morning, change into coaching gear and perform my duties as a college baseball coach / Change back into my chauffeur attire, and deliver a Mo-X shuttle van of passengers back to Columbia on the 8 PM shuttle / Take a four-hour siesta, and repeat the process.

This daily regimen sacrificed sleep, but at least I was trained to function with one eye open. Babe Ruth would be proud!

Rich Fanning inherited an athletic department that

was in danger of being shut down. All coaches were part-time so recruiting suffered mightily. Most of the programs barely had enough players to field a team, and often used athletes from other sports to avoid forfeiting contests. I was hired in September after school had started, and was informed that three baseball players were suiting up for the men's soccer program. None of the three had EVER played organized soccer and didn't know the rules of the game, let alone comprehend strategic nuances necessary to be competitive. I was enjoying a rare day off as a chauffeur, a week into my Harris-Stowe career, when Rich bolted into my makeshift closet-sized office that I shared with the women's soccer coach and said, "I need a favor." I blindly replied, "Absolutely, what's up?" The volleyball team was ready to depart for a match, but the volleyball coach was missing in action. Yours Truly had become a college volleyball coach! The team consisted of six players, which is the bare minimum to field a squad. We loaded the rental van and the seven of us were on an unlikely mission together. I used the half-hour ride to learn the players' names and get acquainted with my new team. We arrived at McKendree College ten minutes before the match, and the opposing coach was initially befuddled at the coaching change. After my explanation, she shook her head and mumbled, "typical Harris-Stowe." College volleyball is a best three out of five sets, and each set is a race to 25 points. I sat on our bench all by my lonesome, and helplessly watched as we swiftly got our asses kicked the first two sets. My only strategic tactic during my one-game volleyball coaching stint was calling a timeout midway through the third set. Lack of physical conditioning (not a surprise when your leader is MIA on game day), and no available substitutions, left the Lady Hornets gasping for air. My timeout probably saved a player from passing out, but merely delayed the inevitable beating. Ironically, my long-awaited debut as a college head coach came in volleyball and not baseball. My career record still sits at 0-1 as a college volleyball coach.

Basketball season brought more comedic futility. The Harlem Globetrotters are universally beloved, and their career record is over 13,000 wins and only one loss. Games are choreographed akin to professional wrestling, and the one loss was an accident. The Globetrotters primary punching bag is the Washington Generals. The Generals are the butt of all Globetrotter jokes in basketball games that are more entertainment than competition. The Harris-Stowe Hornets in 2003 were the NAIA version of the Washington Generals. Due to injuries and quitters, Women's Basketball had five players on the roster midway through the season. Worse yet, one of the players was six months pregnant. By rule, a team must start a contest with five players on the court, but can play with less than five players after the start of the contest. Harris-Stowe's pregnant player would begin the game on the court for the jump ball, and would immediately walk off the court after the opening tip. Harris-Stowe would then play the rest of the game with four players, and the pregnant player departed the gym and headed home. These efforts left the expectant mother with a zero points per game scoring average, but avoided forfeiture for the Lady Hornets. Referees were forewarned during pre-game about the upcoming head-shaking shenanigans. Men's Basketball might as well have started a pregnant player after compiling one win on the season. Two of the three baseball players that played soccer also played basketball due to a lack of bodies. Those two gentlemen can always tell their grandchildren that they were three-sport college athletes, but they should never share any details with the grandkids. Harris-Stowe Athletics was a shit show on life support, and the baseball program followed suit.

My first team meeting was a dandy! Fifteen cats showed up that were either returning players from an 8-43 squad, or walk-ons that didn't know a damn thing about winning a college baseball game. One of the players was wearing the team cap which featured a hornet as the logo. I attempted to capture my audience and lighten the mood by telling the player my first duty would be to replace the cartoon bumblebee with an HS interlocking logo. The player stoically replied, "We switched to the bumblebee logo because we got tired of opponents seeing HS on our cap, and calling us "**H**orse **S**hit" and "**H**igh **S**choolers" while they were kicking our ass." Wow! One minute into my first team meeting, and I realized that changing the culture of Harris-Stowe Baseball would be a monumental task. The ultimate example of a defeatist mentality is changing the logo on your team cap instead of working to get better. Completing the Stowe wardrobe malfunction were the school colors; turd brown and mustard yellow. Old school San Diego Padres baseball pajamas and UPS uniforms are popular entities that rock this same hideous color scheme. UPS's slogan is "What can brown do for you?" While UPS's brown attire is reliable and hard-working, Harris-Stowe's brown uniform did very little while compiling an 8-43 record! My main objective was to obtain names and phone numbers of all meeting participants because, much like other sports at

Harris-Stowe, I needed every warm body imaginable to field a team. I left my first team meeting as a head coach wondering what in the hell I had gotten myself into!

The Stowe, as many locals know it, is a unique place, to say the least. The campus consisted of only three buildings; the Administrative Building which was a revamped three-story high school, the library, and the performance center (theatre, art studio, and gymnasium). Harris-Stowe resides in crime-riddled Midtown St. Louis. My first team meeting included standard introductions, player expectations, etc.......and a stern reminder for players to ALWAYS lock their vehicle, do not leave valuables in plain sight, and park in a lit area. Campus crime was a nuisance, but many in the Harris-Stowe Administration posed an even greater roadblock to building Harris-Stowe Hornets Baseball. Rich Fanning's campus tour, during my interview, was a forerunner for my two-year stay at The Stowe. He paraded me around the small campus sewn into inner city St. Louis, and introduced me to various school administrators. Most of them reeked with negativity and welcomed me like a case of hemorrhoids during constipation. Eventually Rich and I strolled to the baseball field, which is located on campus. The rundown facility is located on the corner of Market and Compton Streets, and is accompanied by the constant roar of deafening city traffic less than twenty yards from the ballpark. Rich sheepishly said, "I hope you aren't hung up on facilities." I channeled my inner Coach Maines, smiled, and optimistically replied, "Once we recruit some good players, this will be a helluva home field advantage."

Maintaining a baseball field is a labor of love, requires tedious attention to detail, and is a time-consuming burden. Basketball coaches sweep the floor, drop the baskets, and are ready to roll in a climate-controlled environment. Baseball coaches cut the grass, water the field, and perform constant upkeep; while battling Mother Nature's elements. The best groundskeeper, like most occupations, is only as good as their budgeted resources. Harris-Stowe Baseball's facilities budget was ZERO dollars, which resulted in a landfill for a field. The Stowe's baseball complex was not self-contained and was commonly frequented by late-night wanderers. The first order of business every morning was walking the field and collecting debris from last night's festivities. Broken glass, cigarette butts, and candy wrappers were usual trash items; used condoms, dog shit and filthy underwear were "special" discoveries. The dugouts often served as homeless shelters for the locals, and I was occasionally greeted by an unsuspecting occupant. One particular early-morning encounter was memorable. I entered the facility and turned the corner of the third base dugout, where I was greeted by a shaggy, unkempt homeless man chewing a cigarette butt and wearing a Harris-Stowe batting helmet that had been inadvertently left out from the previous day's practice. I proceeded to initiate a rambling conversation with our guest who mumbled that his name was Jeff. The conversation eventually led to me throwing Jeff a round of batting practice on the field as the sun came up. My man's swing was beyond repair, but he exuded joy by taking monster hacks on a college baseball field. Jeff departed The Stowe smiling like a jack o lantern after I handed him ten bucks for breakfast and told him to keep the helmet. I plopped down on the same dugout bench that had just finished serving as my new friend's bed, and laughed my ass off all by myself. It was truly a "did that just happen" moment! Busch Stadium is home to the St. Louis Cardinals and is only located a few miles from The Stowe, but I'm quite certain Tony LaRussa has never fed BP at 6 AM to an imperfect stranger!

I was sitting in my cramped office a few days into the job overwhelmed with the challenges of building Harris-Stowe Baseball. Our first practice was the next day, and a couple of eager players requested a bucket of balls to take batting practice at the field. A few hours passed and the same players reappeared and excitedly proclaimed they had met our assistant coach, who had thrown them endless batting practice while wearing a suit and tie. I explained that an assistant coach had not been hired, and they argued that we indeed had an assistant coach, and he would be at practice tomorrow. I entered the ballpark an hour early for my first practice as a head coach. I was startled to see our mystery assistant coach already present, pulling weeds on the infield, while decked out in a full St. Louis Cardinals uniform, with Gibson and 45 stitched into the back of the uni. My new assistant coach was a bespectacled baseball junkie in his mid-50s, weighed 150 pounds soaking wet, and defined perpetual motion. I introduced myself to Mike Kern, and then hired him as our volunteer coach. Mike served as the Director of Information Technology for the St. Louis Chamber of Commerce, was returning from a meeting, and took a wrong turn when he spotted our players taking batting practice. He pulled his car into the ballpark, and offered to throw BP. Coach Kern's love of the game, and spontaneous gesture, kick-started a lifelong friendship. His future contributions were instrumental in revitalizing Hornets

Baseball. Crazy how a baseball program would be impacted by a computer geek that took a wrong turn!

Mike's eternal energy, attention to detail, and tireless work ethic led me to nickname him "Mad Mike." Passion is a key to success, and Mad Mike demonstrated maniacal passion for the game of baseball. He played in two men's leagues, was the oldest player on both of his teams, while pitching and catching for both teams. Mad Mike prided himself on his fungo skills and always strived to improve. The catcher pop up is the most challenging fungo act for a coach, and is designed for catchers to practice catching pop ups. Many coaches attempt this difficult feat, and most fail miserably. The catcher pop up is the ability to hit a baseball straight up in the air, simulating a hitter popping out to the catcher. Mad Mike routinely spent his lunch break honing his catcher pop up fungo skills by hitting GOLF BALLS straight up in the air, dropping his fungo bat, and then quickly putting on a catcher's mitt to catch his own pop up. He rationalized that if practiced with a golf ball, a baseball would be a piece of cake. Good luck trying this at home! The great Jimmie Reese would have been proud of Mad Mike's dedication to the fungo. Cheers to Baseball and Mike Kern!

A college baseball program typically constructs their season-long plan to coincide with the school's academic calendar. The fall semester is split between on-field practices commonly referred to as "fall ball" (September and October), and off-season strength and conditioning workouts (October through December). Pre-season practice is in January (college baseball's version of big league spring training), and the actual season takes place February through May. This cycle has existed forever and makes no sense considering you take an elongated break between your on-field practice sessions, and schedule your pre-season / season during cold and inclement weather. There is a reason Major League Baseball holds spring training in Florida and Arizona! I realized after a few fall practices that my goal for year one was to field a team, not field a COMPETITIVE team. Halfway through the fall semester, the 15 bodies assembled for the first team meeting had diminished to seven. The attrition stemmed from our players' lack of dedication. Sarcasm alert: Can you believe a coach would have the audacity to require players to report on time for team functions?!! I had a player actually quit because he couldn't believe we were going to practice on Saturdays! Even casual fans know nine players are necessary to field a team, and my active roster was two shy of the minimum. I had two choices for the immediate future of Hornets Baseball: recruit at least two players before the spring semester began in early January or pull the plug on year one and forfeit the season.

Rich Fanning and I agreed that forfeiture of our season would be detrimental to building the baseball program, and yet another negative public relations blemish for the perception of Harris-Stowe Athletics. Oatmeal is better than no meal, bad breath is better than no breath, and recruiting players to a shitty program is better than recruiting players to a forfeited season. Most college students choose a school and begin traditional orientation in late August. Signing players in January is atypical, and a tall task for recruiters, especially one searching for baseball players to attend The Stowe. My first strategy was to recruit from within by posting signs around campus, "If you are interested in playing on the baseball team please contact Coach Munns..." This high school-esque exercise resulted in two prank calls and zero players. I beat the bushes and spent the next two months with my cell phone pinned to my ear searching for players. I stumbled upon Prairie Baseball Academy (PBA), which is a post-high school facility in Lethbridge, Alberta (Canada). PBA is a highly successful organization that recruits roughly 50 players from all over Canada, plays a schedule vs. Canadian colleges, and includes a junior varsity program. The director, Blair Kubicek, and his assistant, Todd Hubka, helped send five of their JV players to join the Hornets in January. A blind date with five Canadians had saved the season! PBA has remained a fertile feeding ground throughout my career. I have taken several recruiting trips to PBA, and have had the privilege to coach many of their players. Cheers to Baseball, Blair Kubicek, and Todd Hubka!

Our five Canadian lifesavers arrived at St. Louis Lambert Airport in January and the Hornets roster nearly doubled. I spent the first week of pre-season practice teaching everybody on the team how to pitch. College baseball programs carry roughly fifteen pitchers on their roster. I had twelve players and THREE pitchers on the roster. I had taught pitching at countless youth camps, and my first week of practice at the Stowe felt like I was once again demonstrating pitching fundamentals to a pack of ten-year-olds.

The first half of the season three players suffered season-ending injuries, which left nine active players to stagger through the second half of our season. Pitching changes mirrored a little league dad making a trip to the mound, barking out who was pitching, and informing other players of their new position. Hornet relievers in 2004 didn't enter from the bullpen, but instead were summoned to the mound from another position. An example of a typical pitching change was sending the pitcher to play shortstop, moving the shortstop to play third base, and bringing the third baseman in to pitch. Our opponent's reaction to the pitcher merry-go-round ranged from stunned silence to unruly bench jockeying. The bad news was we limped home to an 11-47 record. The good news was we never forfeited a game and nobody bitched about playing time!

During my first year at The Stowe, Rich Fanning appointed me Sports Information Director, in addition to serving as the Head Baseball Coach. Despite being technologically challenged, I was grateful because this full-time appointment enabled me to retire as a chauffeur for the second time in my life, and recruit 24/7 to build Harris-Stowe Baseball. The recruiting budget mimicked the facilities budget. Wooing players to an 11-47 program was a daunting task, and even more daunting with ZERO dollars! The master plan was to flip Harris-Stowe into a winner, and land a better head coaching job at another school. My wife agreed for me to use our personal credit card, in lieu of a school credit card which didn't exist, to supplement ordinary recruiting efforts (meals during on-campus visits, fueling my pickup for recruiting trips, etc.). A glimpse of why Sarah Munns received a double toast! My new routine became spending a couple of nights a week in St. Louis to ease the tiresome four-hour round-trip commute. I had good friends living in St. Louis that were kind enough to provide me keys to their homes and adopt the gypsy baseball coach with open arms. Cheers to

Baseball, Donnie Hillerman, Doug, and Annie Holder!

Harris-Stowe Baseball was a reclamation project that was Drexel 2.0. The obstacles were eerily similar; undesirable location, atrocious facilities, and a program in shambles. Due to the local negative reputation, I quickly discovered my best recruiting strategy was contacting players from outside the area that were completely unfamiliar with Harris-Stowe Baseball. While the 2004 Hornets were bumbling through a 47-loss season, I had my eye on building the 2005 Hornets. We were playing our final conference series of the 2004 season at home and had been mathematically eliminated from postseason contention. In Major League Baseball this futile act of playing meaningless games late in a season is referred to as "playing out the string." Our opponent was a fellow cellar-dweller in the conference standings, and also had been mathematically eliminated. We split an eyesore of a doubleheader on Friday and were scheduled to play again Saturday afternoon. Friday night brought rain, and Saturday more rain was in the forecast. I made the premeditated executive decision late Friday night that I would cancel our game, and spend my Saturday recruiting junior college baseball in Chicago. I departed St. Louis at 5:00 AM and was three hours into my voyage to Chicago when I called the opposing coach who was eating breakfast at his hotel, "Good morning, this is Coach Munns. We got a lot of rain last night. I'm at the field and it's too wet. Hate to do it, but I'm going to have to cancel our game today." He quickly agreed, ready for his hapless season to be over, and the 2004 Hornets season fittingly ended in a rainout. Mother Nature wreaks havoc every spring on college baseball coaches and is usually a problematic bitch. In this case, she was an absolute sweetheart!

The impromptu trip to Chicago, thanks to Mother Nature, introduced me to Jerry Hodges. Jerry was a standout player at Kankakee Community College, located just outside of Chicago, and was wrapping up an All-American season. Pre-game batting practice is a critical part of the evaluation process when recruiting a hitter, especially when it's the first time seeing that hitter. During a nine-inning game, hitters typically get four or five plate appearances. The recruiter is at the mercy of the opposing pitcher throwing strikes, and the opponent cooperating to enable the hitter to showcase his skills during the actual game. While at Drexel, we hosted Northeastern University who was led by Carlos Pena, their first baseman and future first-round draft pick. 25-30 scouts lined the backstop enduring a steady cold drizzle, to lay their eyes on the future 2009 American League home run leader. We proceeded to walk Pena four times, piss off a gaggle of drenched scouts, and win an important conference game. Those scouts that missed pre-game BP were really pissed off! Unlike other sports, the nature of an actual baseball game can render little benefit to an evaluator. My first impression of Jerry Hodges during pre-game BP was "love at first sight," and no way in hell can I convince this hitting machine to become a Hornet. He was a natural hitter who diligently worked at his craft, and his teammates gravitated toward him. For good measure, Jerry put on an extra base hit display when it counted, played third base like a gold-glover, and led his team to victory. Major League Baseball's pre-game BP begins at 5:00 before a 7:00 game. Hitters that perform during BP but fail to produce in the actual game earn the dubious distinction as

"5:00 hitters." Jerry Hodges hit at 5:00, 7:00, and any other time he waggled a bat. Stay tuned for more to come regarding Mr. Hodges. Unfortunately, my recruiting efforts, much like the trip to Chicago, was accumulating credit card debt, but not accumulating good players.

The calendar was creeping through mid-May and I had only signed four recruits. I feared that my first shot at being a college head baseball coach would result in colossal failure, as the clock ticked to sign twenty players in the next three months. I had grown accustomed to the NCAA Division 1 recruiting timeline, and failed to realize that the NAIA's timeline is much later in nature. Division 1 programs sign players a year, and sometimes two years, in advance of their arrival to campus. The NAIA is a fallback plan for players if they don't get offered, or don't qualify academically, to play NCAA Division 1 baseball. The NAIA's academic requirements are much more lenient than the NCAA's, and thus the NAIA reluctantly becomes plan B for many players. June, July, and August is a feeding frenzy for NAIA baseball programs to bolster their rosters. Good junior college players started signing up to be Hornets and I was finally seeing the fruits of my labor. Endorphins are self-produced opioids in the human body, and when released they cause euphoria. The term "endorphin drip" describes the release of endorphins created because a person has achieved optimal personal satisfaction. A recruiter landing a really good player elicits their endorphin drip much like a gambler hitting a big wager, or a traveler visiting their favorite vacation destination.

By late summer a quality recruiting class had been assembled, but I was still attempting to lure Jerry Hodges to visit The Stowe. My persistent pestering, and offer to attend a St. Louis Cardinals game, sealed the deal for a visit. I am not a believer in fortune tellers, palm readers, or soothsayers; but my inner Nostradamus was certain that Jerry enjoying a memorable visit to St. Louis impacted the future success of Harris-Stowe Baseball. Therefore, I rolled out the red carpet, or in our case the turd brown and mustard yellow carpet, for his visit. I connected immediately with Jerry and his father; great people that are passionate baseball fans. Our trip to Busch Stadium felt like a reunion of three long-time buddies instead of an initial recruiting visit. Jerry signed with the Hornets, and a quality recruiting class became a stellar recruiting class. The term "alpha dog" is high praise for a team leader and signifies a blend of dominating performance and confident (borderline cocky) personality that motivates teammates to follow the alpha dog. Jerry Hodges, known to teammates as Hodgy, talked the talk and backed it up with his play. The self-proclaimed Crusher produced video game numbers his junior season at The Stowe, terrorizing NAIA pitching to the tune of a .492 batting average, 13 home runs, and twenty doubles, which earned him First-Team All American status.

Vision is inexplicably overlooked, yet the most important attribute, when dissecting a hitter. Hodgy had eyes like Superman. Hitters have less than half a second to diagnose the type of pitch, and its' location, before deciding to swing at the pitch. Baseball doesn't feature natural athleticism compared to other sports, but great hitters are masters at hand-eye coordination. Our indoor hitting facility was an undersized gym in the administrative building that was barely capable of housing one batting cage. The length of our batting cage was fifty-six feet and regulation distance from the pitcher's mound to home plate is sixty feet six inches. The gym was painted bright canary yellow, which is a blinding background for a hitter facing live pitching. There is a reason the background beyond centerfield at Major League stadiums is dark green. I invited local pro players to practice with us during our pre-season in January and February. I philosophize that being in the presence of talented players makes you a better player, and I have continued to invite pro players to our practices my entire career for this reason. A Cincinnati Reds farmhand joined our indoor practice to throw a bullpen, but was not scheduled to face any hitters. The right-handed hurler was 6'6", his fastball sat in the mid-90s, and he was just as likely to feed a fastball behind your head as paint the outside corner for a strike. Hodgy pleaded with me to hit against him, and I finally foolishly relented to allow our meal ticket to take hacks vs. a loose cannon at 56 feet, with piss poor sightlines. Hodgy proceeded to line the first fastball he saw off the back of the cage for what would have been a sure extra base hit. I smiled and exhaled all at the same time. Not a bad July signing that originally stemmed from a rainout! Thanks again Mother Nature and cheers to Baseball and Jerry Hodges!

In all, twenty-four new players who were predominantly junior college transfers completed the extreme makeover. Our roster was a diverse melting pot consisting of African-Americans, Mexican-Americans, Caucasians, and Canadians; many of whom arrived with off-field baggage and were grateful for a second chance / last chance. One of college athletics' greatest dynamics, similar to our military branches, is uniting all walks of life from vast cultural backgrounds. Planning for the fall semester included organizing the usual class schedules, practice schedules, strength and conditioning schedules, and the not-so-usual parole officer schedules. One of the few lessons I learned from my Physical Education coursework at Missouri Western was, "as a teacher, never let the kids see you smile until after Christmas." This lesson was applicable for the 2005 Hornets. Aside from coaching the game of baseball, I spent much of the fall semester busting their ass to make responsible decisions off the field, and buy into team initiatives. My eyes were opened after our first team meeting. The baseball office was located in the gym and was approximately 100 yards from the baseball field. I was carrying two buckets of balls to the field and a player asked if I wanted a lift. A kind gesture for sure, but upon grabbing the shotgun seat in his vehicle, I couldn't help but notice a half-drank longneck bottle of beer in the cup holder, and a lit cigarette in the ashtray. I intentionally overlooked the obvious party fouls, and couldn't wait to begin the Harris-Stowe Baseball voyage.

The first player to report to our inaugural fall practice was a stocky right-handed pitcher named Craig McAndrews. Craig was from Omaha, Nebraska and had just completed a successful two-year career at Southwestern Iowa Community College before signing with the Hornets. Players were issued a practice t-shirt and team cap but had to supply their own practice pants. Craig rocked navy blue pinstriped baseball pajamas that were perfectly knee-high crimped and could have passed for one of Babe Ruth's old-school pajama bottoms. His navy stirrups were stretched evenly in length and exemplified proper appearance for a baseball player. Not surprising, considering he was mentored by his high school coach, and Omaha legend, John Stella. Coach Stella is still coaching and throwing batting practice at eighty-five years young. He is cut from the same cloth as Zim, Red, and Jimmie Reese. Cheers to Baseball and John Stella!

Craig's punctuality and attention to baseball attire were a precursor for things to come. I told him I liked his pins and how he wore the uniform, and he replied he was a big-time Yanks fan because his uncle played for the Bronx Bombers. David "Boomer" Wells was a mainstay in the Yankees rotation at the time, and Craig was a miniature version. I promptly issued him the nickname Boomer and predicted to myself he would be a leader in our program. The Harris-Stowe Boomer was South Omaha tough, competitive as hell, and the glue for our band of renegades. My first impression of Craig's leadership capabilities was accurate. He was a key cog in the Hornets bullpen, but more importantly, he became a lifelong friend that has served as my assistant coach the past fifteen seasons. The nickname also stuck; much like Yogi and Ichiro in Major League Baseball, he is a one-name legend in college baseball circles. Many players and coaches revere Boomer but have never heard of Craig McAndrews. Years after Craig was nicknamed Boomer, we were attending the national baseball coaches' convention in Nashville. Our convention, like all "professional" development gatherings, doubles as a three-day vacation/party. We were conducting a late evening "clinic" at Tootsies bar with some coaching buddies and one of them said, "David Wells was in here last night, but he wouldn't talk to anybody or sign any autographs." I personally don't blame David Wells, or any other famous person, for requesting privacy in public. However, I bet each of the coaches a beer that I would get a picture of the two Boomers if David Wells reappeared at Tootsies. The key to sustaining initial conversation with a celebrity is making it personal, succinct, and genuinely flattering. David Wells strolled into Tootsies and I took my best shot, "Hey Boomer, I was at old Yankee Stadium, game one of the '98 World Series, when you entered to Van Halen's *Running with the Devil.* I coach college baseball and nicknamed this guy next to me Boomer because he's a huge Yanks fan and a big-game pitcher. Can we get a real quick picture?" The original Boomer shot me a stunned glance, took a picture with my buddy Boomer, and wished us good luck in our season. Cheers to Baseball and David Wells! Cheers to Baseball and Craig McAndrews!

The 2005 Hornets flipped 11-47 into 34-27, and the 23-win improvement was the largest in all of NAIA Baseball. We advanced to the American Midwest Conference post-season tournament for the first time in school history, and fell one win shy of qualifying for the National Tournament. What began as a cluster of castoffs, misfits, and hooligans became a united band of brothers that played with a chip on their shoulder, and will go down as one of my all-time favorite teams that I have ever coached. Almost the entire team was returning for a promising 2006 season. Sarah Munns permitted me to return for one, and only ONE, more season at The Stowe with a single stipulation; our personal credit card would no longer serve as the school's credit card. A reasonable request to say the least, and besides, recruiting was pointless since 2006 was definitely my Stowe swan song. I was either being spit back into the real world or landing another coaching job. My next coaching opportunity came sooner than anticipated. A month into the fall semester I was contacted by William Woods University whose head coach had unexpectedly resigned. William Woods is a NAIA school located a half-hour from my home in Columbia, and merely shaving three hours from my daily commute made the job enticing. I interviewed and was offered the job to become William Woods' next head coach.

Sane individuals would have immediately accepted the position, but loyalty temporarily trumped sanity and I asked for a day to ponder my decision. Like most people that are considering a job change, I created my pros and cons list and it was almost unanimously slanted toward accepting the new position. William Woods was superior in every category pertinent to running a college baseball program, but the one powerful Harris-Stowe edge was the players I would be leaving behind. Job loyalty is foreign to professionals in the majority of industries because the human element is not directly involved. Team loyalty is a different animal due to the family-like attachment that is developed in a program that prioritizes relationships ahead of selfish career motives. College Athletics is loaded with nomadic creatures that operate without a conscience while job jumping. I agonized over the decision but finally decided accepting the William Woods job was my best chance at remaining a college baseball coach beyond the 2006 season. If my Harris-Stowe experience was a MasterCard commercial it would read like this:

* Recruiting a college baseball team: $12,000 in credit card debt.

* Gas for the four-hour round-trip to work: thousands more dollars.

* One BP session with Jeff: PRICELESS!

# Chapter Three:
## Meet "The Whizzanator"

Darren Munns
Head Baseball Coach
William Woods University
October 2005 – June 2015

"Do you have your CDL?" was the first question asked by Athletics Director, Larry York, BOTH times I interviewed for the William Woods job. I had flashbacks that I was interviewing to be a chauffeur again, rather than as a college baseball coach. The CDL (Commercial Driver's License) was as critical as your baseball acumen, coaching philosophy, or ability to recruit good players; because the coach was also the bus driver for all road trips. Hiring a coach that can drive a bus is essential when budgets are too tight to contract a bus company. The first time I interviewed for the Woods job, I was out of coaching and driving a shuttle van. To say I was a long shot to land the job would be an understatement considering all the other candidates were actually coaching college baseball, and not claiming occupation in ground transportation. However, I nailed the interview and felt optimistic about my chances to become the next Head Baseball Coach at William Woods. I drove off campus excited that my return to college baseball was inevitable, and anxiously awaited a call that never came.

Unfortunately, I was the bridesmaid and another quality candidate was hired to lead the William Woods baseball program. Anybody that has had their heart set on a job understands the disappointment when they are not the chosen one. Failing to land a job after nailing an interview is like a kid who doesn't get his dream gift after opening his last present on Christmas morning, or a poker player who suffers a "bad beat" when they are sure their hand is a winner. I subsequently was hired at Harris-Stowe, who is in the same conference as William Woods. It was clearly apparent, during my interview sequel at William Woods three years later, that my hiring was a foregone conclusion. I was offered the position before I left campus. At one point during the committee portion of my interview, which included several players, a William Woods player stated that they had a full-time strength coach which gave them an advantage vs. their competition. I replied, "At Harris-Stowe most of the weights were stolen from our weight room, you are looking at our strength coach, and last season our Harris-Stowe team beat you four out of five games, including a win in the conference tournament that ended your season." The competitive bastard in me could not resist taking a subtle jab at the competition. The moral to the story: Never burn a bridge and use rejection as your motivational fuel.

Larry York is an old school disciplinarian that is a member of multiple athletic Hall of Fames, and played football for the legendary coach, Dan Devine, at the University of Missouri. "Firm, fair and consistent" was his mantra, and he excelled in conflict resolution. I grew to respect Larry because he always had your back when dealing with a student-athlete, faculty member, parent, or anybody else that dared to cast wrongful accusations. He actually looked forward to conflict resolution, whereas many administrators cowardly sidestep defending their coaching staff. Cheers to Baseball and Larry York! While the William Woods Owls program had many challenges, the starting line was a layup compared to The Stowe. I inherited a 19-40 team; better than 8-47. The budgets were challenging; better than no budgets at all. There was a full roster of players; better than barely having enough players to field a team. William Woods Baseball, like the vast majority of small college athletic programs, was insufficiently funded and required mass fundraising to survive. It is a cruel irony that the word "fun" represents the first three letters in the words **fun**draising and **fun**eral.

The previous coach had organized a fundraiser to work the concession stands at St. Louis Blues home hockey games. On my first day on the job, our Graduate Assistant Coach, Josh Swenson, who I adopted upon taking the job, informed me we were going to the Blues game tonight. Josh was an intelligent young lad that played at William Woods, and was a tremendous help for me transitioning to The Woods. Cheers to Baseball and Josh Swenson! I thought, "I'm going to like my new assistant. He's a sports fan, and is insistent on us bonding by attending a hockey game together." That was before I knew the Blues game was a **fun**draiser and not a **fun** trip. My first day on the job was spent driving a van full of players to a Blues game for an evening of fundraising. So much for escaping the four-hour round-trip to St. Louis! I quickly discontinued the Blues fundraiser and partnered with Mizzou Athletics to work their football and basketball games. Although the players still had a miserable experience, at least the commute shrunk from two hours to twenty minutes. Raffles, 50/50 tickets, outfield sign sponsors, hosting youth baseball tournaments, and hosting an annual golf tournament also made the list of necessary nuisances to keep Owls Baseball afloat. These fundraising efforts were time-consuming weekend killers, but the runaway frontrunner for fundraising frustration was working the NASCAR race at Kansas Motor Speedway. The mere mention of the word "NASCAR" makes Owls alumni swear out loud in disgust; social distancing is recommended in case they vomit at the thought of NASCAR. The itinerary for this annual headache was as follows:

- Load the bus Saturday morning at 2:00 AM
- Coach Munns drives the bus while every player sleeps
- Arrive at Kansas Motor Speedway for check-in at 5:00 AM
- Assist with food set up, deliver food to suites all day, clean the suites after the race
- Load the bus at 9:00 PM
- Coach Munns repeats step two and we arrive home at midnight

That's a day you will never get back! I made an executive decision, after the first couple of NASCAR nightmares, to at least enhance my personal experience. A casino is conveniently located approximately two miles from the racetrack. Once all players were registered to spar with NASCAR, I informed my assistant coaches to call me if there were any issues, and I hiked to a blissful day of blackjack and poker. Before you think less of the author: I justified spending the day scratching my gambling itch since I was chauffeuring thirty-five comatose bodies to and from this traumatic experience known to Owls alumni as simply "NASCAR." While nonstop fundraising was a royal pain in the ass for our players, and an accounting migraine for the head coach; the ongoing, yet necessary, irritation paled in comparison to the lack of team chemistry that I inherited. Team chemistry is an overused phrase that is usually spoken without proper and thorough analysis. I am a staunch believer that team chemistry is the most vital component to build a successful team, and plays a prominent factor in the outcome of equal, or even close-to-equal, combatants. Individual exit meetings between coaches and players are commonplace in college baseball programs at the end of fall ball and upon completion of the spring season. They are an opportunity to discuss all things coach/player. "How is our team chemistry?" is prioritized as the FIRST question I ask every player during their exit meeting.

The first team meeting at William Woods could have served as an infomercial for negative body language. I began the meeting by informing the group that yawning would get you immediately dismissed. Yawning is the ultimate disrespectful act and indicates a person is disinterested in the message. A team expectation of mine has always been for coaches and players to not yawn while communicating with one another. Ten minutes into my first meeting two players had been dismissed for yawning. The group collectively was slumped in chairs and the majority had an "F U" look about them, and displayed a "players vs. coaches" mindset. Taking over in the middle of fall semester is an inopportune time to be hired because you hit the ground running with players that somebody else recruited. My message on day one, to hopefully retain players, was asking each player to give me one week of practice to earn their trust, and then they could make a decision to stay or transfer to another school. I also extended an optional invitation for any player to stop by the baseball office the next day to discuss their situation, and provide any thoughts regarding the team. My Mom always told me, "you have two ears and one mouth, you should listen twice as much as you talk."

My ears were wide open as players stopped by the office to point fingers at teammates, blame the previous coach, and make excuses for last season. Negativity and excuses are the tools for losers, but in this case, I was thankful for the players' input because my new team unknowingly helped me gauge our team chemistry. The first week I dismissed a player for stealing equipment, dismissed another player for visiting other schools behind my back, and dismissed several more players for flat out not being coachable. A newcomer to the program was a junior college All-American infielder that could really hit, but was lazy (we will refer to him moving forward as Captain Lazy). He was also allergic to playing defense. Pitching and defense are the staple of any successful team, but most players would rather hit all day than work on their defense. "Pitching and defense wins games" is my constant reminder for any team I coach. Coaches that have run an instructional youth baseball camp, quickly discover that hitting is the last fundamental you practice at camp. All kids love to hit, and by making hitting last on the camp agenda, you have a greater chance of holding their attention span throughout camp. During our first fall practice, after I reviewed and demonstrated a proper infield stance, I began hitting the infielders ground balls. Each infielder was diligently practicing the fundamentals that I had just taught them, busting their ass to make a great first impression on the new coach, until it was Captain Lazy's turn. A good infielder's stance resembles a dog taking a dump; knees bent, hands out in front of the body, head down, and fierce concentration. You will never look at an infielder or a dog taking a dump the same way again! Captain Lazy decided to be the class clown and field his groundball with his glove between his legs and behind his legs. After I jumped his ass, he explained he always does that on his first groundball. I hit him another groundball and he repeated the same trick, then told me, "This drill is little league bullshit and I hit .500 last season." I replied, "I don't care if you hit a thousand, get your ass out of practice and come see me tomorrow morning." Captain Lazy's career as an Owl was short-lived, and he was dismissed the next morning. Team chemistry reigns supreme at all times!

After taking the team temperature for a week, and trimming the cancer, it was time to build our team. The previous coach had signed a promising recruiting class and there was existing talent already in the program. Players bought into team initiatives and we flipped last year's 19-40 debacle into a successful 34-18 season. I spent the next decade as the coach at William Woods, and there were plenty of accolades for Owls Baseball; we graduated 90% of our players, had a retention rate in the 90th percentile, averaged 34 wins per season, finished in the top three of the conference standings every season, qualified for the semi-finals of the conference tournament every season, and appeared in eight of ten conference championship games. Personally, during my Woods tenure I learned valuable leadership lessons, and habitually practiced self-analysis to become a better leader. My top revelations (after much thought) were delegating more to assistant coaches and team leaders, smile at your players when they fail in their biggest moments, involve EVERY team member EVERY day, and believe in your process. Process is a popular sports catchphrase thanks to Bill Belichick frequently mumbling process while leading the New England Patriots dynasty, the Philadelphia 76ers rebuild was deemed a process, and the Houston Astros massive overhaul from MLB joke to World Series champion followed a calculated process (famously predicted by *Sports Illustrated* and displayed on their cover). *SI* would have really impressed if they prognosticated the Astros elaborate pitch stealing system that tainted their World Series championship. You will hear much more about the importance of process later in the book, but anybody that preaches process has probably at some point doubted their own process.

I definitely second-guessed the Munns Process after going 0-4 in my first four conference championship games as the Owls skipper. Worse yet, I was 0-3 as a Drexel assistant in championship games, 0-1 as a volunteer assistant at Central Methodist, and had lost a championship game as the skipper of a competitive wood bat summer collegiate league. All told, Yours Truly was 0-9 as a coach in championship games. Holy loser! Dog piles are awesome if you are dog piling, but absolutely suck if you have a front-row seat while watching your opponent dog pile. Baseball players sprinting to a dog pile resembles a contestant on *The Price is Right,* overflowing with uncontrollable excitement, while being summoned to "come on down" to contestant row. It wasn't until we won our first conference championship game that I realized the process was more important than hoisting the trophy. A conference official congratulated me for finally winning a championship game, and asked if I felt like a monkey had been knocked off my back. I instinctively replied, "No, I'm proud of all of our teams that have appeared in championship games." A championship is rewarding, but the margin between winning and losing in a championship game is minuscule. The Owls were 2-6 in championship games during my tenure, and almost every game was decided in the late innings. We lost on a ninth-inning wild pitch, lost in extra innings twice, and won on a ninth-inning home run. A winning program is different than a winning team. A winning program consistently repeats their process, accomplishes similar annual positive results, and has a chance to win every season. A winning team signifies ONE season that a team had success. Many teams come and go, but programs have staying power. Every team's goals are relative to their realistic expectations, and a conference championship loss is just as devastating for athletes and coaches, as a World Series or Super Bowl loss is for those at the highest level. A lifelong lesson I learned from my mentor, Don Maines, was exhibited before Drexel played in their championship games. He always told the team, "regardless of what happens today, I'm proud of you for your efforts and accomplishments this season." This pre-game message is a genuine thank you for their collective efforts, as opposed to making a knee-jerk emotional post-game speech based on one game's outcome.

For years coaches and players in all sports have been judged by titles won, and rightfully so to a degree. Mike

Martin, the long-time Florida State iconic Head Coach, is the poster person for consistently fielding winning teams, but falling short of winning a national championship. Coach Martin is college baseball's all-time winningest coach, and retired with a career record of 2,029-736-4. More amazing, his teams appeared in the post-season for 41 consecutive seasons. **FORTY-ONE CONSECUTIVE SEASONS!!** The Seminoles program is the model for consistency, and Coach Martin is on my Mount Rushmore of college baseball coaches, despite not winning a title. Dorrel Norman Elvert Herzog, better known as Whitey, is my all-time personal favorite baseball figure. The White Rat is a baseball genius that managed the St. Louis Cardinals during the decade of the 1980s, and went 1-2 in World Series appearances. All three of Whitey's World Series were decided in game sevens. In 1985 the Cards lost the I-70 World Series to the cross-state Kansas City Royals, and in 1987 they lost to the Minnesota Twins. Game six, ninth inning, of the '85 Series infamously featured one of the worst calls in the history of sports when first base umpire Don Denkinger called Royals batter/runner Jorge Orta safe when he was clearly out at first base. The blown call led to a Royals rally and eventual World Series title. The '87 Twins played in the Metrodome, and had a decided home-field advantage due to the Dome's white ceiling and deafening acoustics. The '87 Series was the first in history that the home team won every game of a seven-game series. Whitey Herzog's two fewer titles, thanks to a blown call and a circus of a "ballpark," delayed his rightful enshrinement into Cooperstown, but should never lessen his consistent greatness. Should The White Rat be exclusively judged on the outcome of three game sevens?

Gene Mauch is considered one of the greatest baseball minds of all time. Unfortunately, he is more known for coming close, but never winning the big one. Mauch is eighth on the all-time wins list for Major League managers but never won a league pennant. Three times he came within one game of winning the coveted league pennant. He is also associated with some of the greatest collapses in baseball history. His 1964 Phillies team held a 6 ½ game lead with 12 games to play and lost an improbable ten straight games to blow the pennant. In 1982 his California Angels squad became the first team in an MLB five-game playoff series history to blow a 2-0 lead, and lose three straight games to lose the series. His 1986 Angels led the Boston Red Sox 3-1 in the best-of-seven American League Championship Series, and were ONE STRIKE away in game five from clinching a World Series berth when Dave Henderson homered off Halos closer Donnie Moore to send Game Five into extra innings. The Red Sox won Game Five, then the next two games as well, depriving Gene Mauch of finally advancing to the World Series.

Players also lose rank because they lack a strong post-season resume. Ernie Banks, known as "Mr. Cub," had a Hall of Fame career and was voted to the All-Century team. He was obviously one of the greatest players of all time, but he spent his entire career with the bumbling Cubs, and the result was Mr. Cub holding the dubious MLB record for most games played without a post-season appearance (2,528). Angels centerfielder, Mike Trout, is widely recognized as the best player in baseball, and is on pace to become arguably the greatest player in baseball history. In eight full seasons, Trout has won three MVP awards, finished second four times in the MVP voting, and finished fourth one time in the voting. His career .419 on base percentage is video game material! Yet Trout has appeared in only three post-season games, when the Angels were unceremoniously swept by the Kansas City Royals in the 2014 American League Division Series. The fact that the game's best player has participated in three post-season games in eight seasons is a testament that baseball is the ultimate team game, and players should not be solely judged by their post-season credentials. Mr. Trout is only twenty-eight years old and in the prime of his career, so hopefully at some point soon baseball fans will be treated to seeing the game's best player on the game's grandest stage.

There are countless other examples in all sports. Dan Marino, Hall of Fame quarterback of the Miami Dolphins, is one of the greatest to ever take snaps in the NFL, but was 0-1 in Super Bowls. Bud Grant and Marv Levy both coached the Minnesota Vikings and Buffalo Bills respectively, both are Hall of Famers, and both went 0-4 in Super Bowls. Bud Grant stated that he would rather be 0-4 than 0-0. Marv Levy lost his first of four consecutive Super Bowls when Scott Norwood's last-second field goal narrowly missed wide right. Do you think differently of Marv Levy if Norwood's field goal was good and the Bills were Super Bowl champs? Dean Smith is one of the most successful college basketball coaches of all time. Coach Smith led the University of North Carolina for thirty-six seasons amassing an incredible 879-254 record. Yet it wasn't until his 21$^{st}$ season, and seventh Final Four appearance, that he finally won a national championship when Michael Jordan hit a game-winning jump shot with under twenty seconds to play. It took the greatest basketball player to ever walk the planet sinking a late jumper for Dean Smith to finally win a national championship. Winning and losing is fickle by nature when the two combatants are equal or nearly equal. However, if the leader has a proven process in place, their team will consistently have an annual shot at winning a title.

Attempting to win baseball titles at William Woods was a small piece of my job description. Coaches usually wear many hats when employed by small colleges. While serving as the Owls skipper I also taught classes, was the bus driver for other sports, served as play-by-play broadcaster for men's and women's home basketball games, and was a member of the athletic department's drug screening committee. My role on the drug screening committee was to serve as a witness when a male athlete pissed in a cup to provide his urine sample. The male athlete and I would step into the restroom and he would pee in the cup with me present. I certainly was not a complete "cock hawk," but the process was nonetheless awkward for both parties. The screenings were performed early in the morning, and approximately a dozen athletes were randomly selected a couple of times a semester to be tested. One particular morning a male athlete was clearly attempting to circumvent the system. He had stage fright and could not pee in the cup, then wasn't feeling well, then more stage fright. This charade continued for an hour, and Larry York was getting more perturbed by the minute. A nurse always administered the screening and took the temperature of all samples to verify they were legitimate. Finally, the male athlete produced a sample, but the temperature of his urine indicated the sample was tainted. Larry, myself, and Barry Doty (our Head Golf Coach) joined the male athlete in the hallway outside the training room. Larry questioned his sample and interrogated him for a few minutes, basically calling "bullshit" that the male athlete had actually pissed in the cup. The guilty youngster finally had enough, dropped his sweatpants around his ankles, and yelled "suck it!" My immediate reaction was that we were subjected to either a prosthetic penis or strap-on sex toy, but instead, we had an unforgettable surprise encounter with The Whizzanator! Larry burst into a "gotcha" cackle, and my man's Whizzanator had failed him. Cheers to Baseball and Barry Doty, who joined me to witness the William Woods Whizzanator!

I learned many valuable coaching lessons during my ten years at the helm of Owls Baseball. The most impactful lesson came from Gordie Gillespie, one of the greatest coaches of all time. Coach Gillespie was a gentle giant that coached high school football, college basketball and college baseball for 58 years. His win/loss record was outstanding in all three sports (224-54-6 in high school football, 220-117 in college basketball, and 1,893-952-2 in college baseball). His mission as a coach was even better than his stellar win/loss record. I met Coach Gillespie while he was coaching at the University of St. Francis, a NAIA school near Chicago. We were scheduled to play St. Francis three times on our annual spring break trip to Daytona Beach, FL. At the time, Coach Gillespie was in his 80s and toward the end of an illustrious career. He was extremely modest considering all of his accomplishments and was more interested in getting to know me than talking about his own program. We both had solid teams, and in our first two games we split very competitive extra-inning games. A few days later we were scheduled to play our third game. I attempted to motivate our team by claiming we had a tremendous opportunity to win the three-game series vs. a really good team. Both teams were playing their final game before leaving Daytona.

Coach Gillespie and I exchanged lineups before our game, and I immediately noticed that his starting lineup was nine completely different players from the first two times we had played them. My first thought was his best players succumbed to the temptations of Daytona Beach, and were being benched for conduct detrimental to the team. We won a 10-0 laugher vs. St. Francis' backup players, and I strolled across the field for the customary post-game handshake with the opposing coach. The conversation went something like this:

Coach Gillespie said, "Good luck this season Darren. You guys have a great team."

I thanked Coach Gillespie for the compliment and wished him the very best. As we began to walk away I couldn't resist asking him the obvious, "Coach, I have to ask, you clearly played a completely different lineup than the first two games we played. Any reason for playing the new lineup?"

Coach Gillespie replied, "Darren do you guys fund-raise?"

I quickly replied, "We fundraise a ton."

Coach Gillespie administered the lesson I will never forget, "We fundraise for our spring break trip. Every year the final game of our trip, I play all the guys that haven't gotten to play during the trip. They deserve to play if they put in the work to pay for the trip."

Wow! One of the most accomplished coaches of all time, with a jillion wins on his resume, valued his players experience over one game. The best part of the story is Coach Gillespie's humbleness. The only reason he shared that he played his backups was because I asked about his new lineup. He was not about to downgrade our victory or make an excuse for his team's poor play. Coach Gillespie passed away in 2015, but his influence lives on. Thanks for the lesson Coach Gillespie. Cheers to Baseball and Gordie Gillespie!

o o o o o o o o

Columbia College had been a highly successful NAIA athletic department for years. They only had five sports, but all five sports competed at the national level, were fully funded, and were well supported. During my tenure at William Woods it was frequently rumored that Columbia College would add baseball. I was constantly asked by other coaches, friends, and people in the community, 'Would you be interested in the Columbia College job if they add baseball?' Finally in the summer of 2015 Columbia College announced they were adding Baseball. I had spent a decade building William Woods Baseball and we were coming off back-to-back 39-win seasons (39-12 and 39-14), but the challenge of building another program enticed me to interview for the job. My life, and William Woods Baseball, was on cruise control. On July 1, 2015, I accepted the position at Columbia College, and on July 3, 2015, my first and only child was born. Cheers to Baseball and Mary Ellen Munns! Cruise control switched to full speed ahead! Thanks to my William Woods experience I will never attend another NASCAR race, and I had the privilege to meet The William Woods Whizzanator!

# Chapter Four:
# From Homeless to a Dog Pile

Darren Munns
Head Baseball Coach
Columbia College
July 2015 – Present

During the "do you have any questions for us" portion of my interview at Columbia College (CC), I instantly asked, "Is our program required to fundraise?" Bob Burchard was a Hall of Fame basketball coach, who also served as Athletics Director, and had built the Columbia College Athletic Department into a NAIA powerhouse. As impressive was his glorious Hall of Fame mustache. For reference, similar famous sports mustaches include pro golfer Craig "The Walrus" Stadler, NFL coaching giant Andy Reid, and the late great racing legend Dale Earnhardt. As a man who is only capable of a Larry Bird-esque peach fuzz mustache, I tip my cap to those that sprout a full-fledged caterpillar between their nostrils and upper lip. Coach Burchard replied to my fundraising question, "We don't do bake sales at Columbia College." Music to my ears! I left the interview aroused at the thought of not fundraising while operating a college baseball program. Cheers to Baseball and Bob Burchard!

After being offered the head coaching position at

Columbia College, I once again drew up my pros and cons list. The list was slanted toward CC, but there were several challenging variables to consider. I would be given a full year to recruit a team before the program began playing games. This strategy allowed the program to compete at a high level immediately, but I would not have an assistant coach in year one. How badly does a man want to leave an established program, coming off consecutive 39-win seasons, to put himself through the rigors of recruiting a full roster in one year, with no assistance? The answer is a man that was absolutely sick of fundraising! My other reservation was the facility situation for the brand new baseball program at CC. There was no facility! Columbia College is landlocked in center city Columbia, MO, and the only way to build is up. It was revealed to me during my interview that an off-campus facility would have to be secured, and the chosen head coach would assist with the process. Most coaches would find it baffling that a school would start a baseball program without any facilities, but thanks to my past experiences with shoddy facilities, I didn't bat an eye at starting a homeless program.

No team, no field, no problem! My first duty as the Head Baseball Coach at Columbia College was an introductory press conference which signified a baseball program at CC. Bob Burchard opened the proceedings by informing the media that we have a coach, but we don't have a field. His comment sparked chuckles from the local media, and most of them probably assumed he was joking. After all, who in the hell would start a college baseball program with no field! The famous line from the classic baseball movie *Field of Dreams* was, "If you build it, they will come." Columbia College Baseball hadn't found a field, let alone built one, but they had hired a crazy ass coach willing to take a leap of faith. Having lived in Columbia for nearly twenty years, I was familiar with all potential baseball facilities. Upon my recommendation, CC partnered with the City of Columbia and secured the only facility that had college dimensions, which was a city complex located fifteen minutes from campus that became our "home" facility. The five-field complex is constructed entirely of chain link fencing. The Chain Link Jungle was ideal for youth league tournaments, but was a tough sell as a legitimate college yard to potential recruits, especially being a fifteen-minute commute from campus. I didn't have time to dwell on facilities because the clock was ticking to sign good players. My task was a familiar one; recruit an entire roster in fifteen months. Mary Ellen Munns had other ideas!

My bride and I had waited fifteen years and were finally an induced labor from the birth of our first child. Although practicing for more than a decade was thrilling, not slipping the puck past the goalie was frustrating. Much like baseball, childbirth can be unpredictable. My father-in-law is one of fourteen children. My brother has four kids, and every time he breathed on his wife she got pregnant. Genetics were highly in our favor, but we were a family anomaly. After sitting bedside for ten hours, and as morning approached, I asked the nurse, "Is it OK if I walk two blocks to the grocery store to grab a newspaper?" The nurse replied, "Sure, it will be at least five or six more hours before we are ready for delivery." As I walked into the store, Sarah called my cell phone and informed me the baby had gone sideways and she was being rushed to the delivery room. Our future daughter's wayward activity in the womb was like a base runner that cannot decide between sliding feet first or head first. Caught in between these two options usually results in a crash landing. Please put the book down for a moment and Google "David Palmer slide," to witness the worst slide in MLB history. Seriously, don't read any further until viewing the "David Palmer slide." Ouch! Thankfully, Mary Ellen Munns did not mimic Mr. Palmer as she entered the world! I arrived in time to see the long-awaited birth of our daughter, and building Columbia Cougar Baseball had been delayed due to this life-changing event.

Time to recruit! I was assigned an office the size of a dorm room that was located on the second floor of a converted rundown duplex, which housed five other coaches' offices. However, elaborate campus headquarters were unnecessary because my ass was hitting the road in search of 35-40 players, and would not be spending much time in the baseball office. I generally spent Monday through Wednesday hosting campus visits and recruited off campus Thursday through Sunday. High school players were extremely interested in a start-up program, figuring they would have a greater chance to play immediately than if they joined an established program. The junior college players were skeptical of signing with a brand new program, and they presented an even greater challenge than usual as an NAIA program. I hung a dry erase board in my office to track our signed recruits, which is standard practice for college coaches of all sports. On my first day on the job, I stared at a blank dry erase board knowing the chore that lied ahead of me. The board slowly but surely accumulated forty under-recruited players that predomi- nantly fit one of the following three descriptions; the overlooked high school player, the junior college player that did not qualify academically for the NCAA, and the junior college player that had a poor juco career but I believed had untapped potential. The highest praise received as a NAIA coach is in the form of a question: "How in the hell did you get him?" Three of the most successful players from our inaugural recruiting class all came with their own unique recruiting stories. The following recount for each player proves recruiting is a combination of timing, luck and having the Contrarian onions to believe in a player when nobody else does.

Mark Haire was about to begin his senior year of high school, and he was one of the best left-handed pitchers in the St. Louis area. I had followed Mark's career, but I wanted to see him pitch one more time before making him an offer. We arranged a bullpen session at an indoor facility, and I showed up bearing down on the big lefty with a radar gun in hand. Mark introduced me to his high school teammate that was going to catch his bullpen. Kenny Piper was an undersized athletic catcher not being recruited by any four-year schools, and was also heading into his senior season. Shortly after the bullpen session Mark signed with the Cougars, and recommended I see Kenny play because he also had an interest in CC. Kenny was playing in a fall league, and I attended one of his games the following week with low expectations. My mood quickly changed after seeing Kenny's advanced skill set, competitive demeanor, and how hard he played. I spoke with him and his family after the game and invited them for a campus visit. Kenny called when he arrived on campus and said he and his Mom were in front of the main building. I walked across campus to find him and his Mom playing catch on the front lawn of the school. In almost three decades of hosting recruits, this is the only recruit/Mom game of catch I have witnessed. A true baseball family! Kenny soon signed to become a Cougar, and after signing his Mom sheepishly asked if Kenny could wear uniform number six because his favorite player was Stan Musial. I was sold on a recruit that was a helluva player, valued his family, and revered Stan the Man! Kenny put on thirty good pounds, was conference Freshman of the Year, earned All-American honors his sophomore and junior years, and was drafted in the 18th round by the Tampa Bay Rays following his junior season. By the way, he was gladly issued number six! I'm glad I decided to see Mark Haire pitch one more time! Mark is a great person that cracked our conference rotation during his junior and senior seasons, and he also inadvertently contributed mightily to the future of CC Baseball by recommending his buddy. Cheers to Baseball, Mark Haire, and Kenny Piper!

Chris Wall resembled a baby giraffe on ice skates the first time I saw him pitch. I was perched at a showcase event along with 40-50 other college coaches on the hunt for players. There are far more suspects than prospects showcasing their "skills" at these events. In this particular showcase, each pitcher faced four hitters. Chris proceeded to walk all four hitters he faced, and every coach in attendance BUT ONE scratched him off their list. My menu of fetishes includes a good poker game, fantasy football drafts, sipping a smooth cocktail while listening to music on my deck, and left-handed pitchers. Although Chris' fastball velocity didn't register a number that would get you pulled over by a highway patrolman, he was 6'6" and left-handed. Like many tall young pitchers, he hadn't learned to coordinate his top and bottom half throughout the process of his delivery. All evaluators can differentiate between a polished player and a poor player, but the true art of player evaluation is the ability to project a prospect. I called Chris after his disastrous showcase outing, and he informed me no other schools had contacted him. Perfect! Chris signed to become a Cougar and the rest is history. He has ascended from an unfinished project as a freshman to possessing a 90 mile per hour fastball and becoming our staff ace his sophomore and junior season; which included 17 wins in 17 starts, and over two strikeouts per inning pitched. Chris shockingly did not get drafted after his junior season, and transferred (with my blessing) to the University of Missouri to pitch his senior season in the Southeastern Conference, which is arguably the best Division 1 baseball conference in the country. His rise to dominance can be attributed to his work ethic and tireless pursuit of excellence. Chris is as dedicated to the craft of pitching as any hurler I have ever coached. Quite an accomplishment for a guy that couldn't record an out in a showcase! Cheers to Baseball and Chris Wall!

When something is too good to be true, a person usually winds up thoroughly disappointed. I kept waiting for that moment while recruiting Andrew Warner, and thankfully that moment never came. Andrew, like many juco players, received bad advice and did not prioritize academics, and therefore his only option was attending a NAIA school. He was attending his second junior college (Longview Community College), and the first time I saw him play was in a fall scrimmage. The coaches at Longview were trusted friends of mine and they raved about their catcher/centerfielder, Andrew Warner. Reality exceeded the hype as I watched this man-child (he was 6'3", 240 lbs., and built like a middle linebacker) launch baseballs out of the ballpark to all fields during his rounds of pre-game batting practice. Andrew homered twice during the scrimmage, one of which was a mammoth bomb over the scoreboard that still hasn't landed. His jaw-dropping power display and baseball talent were clearly apparent to even a novice fan, but he demonstrated two intangibles the first day I met him that were equally noteworthy.

Pre-game infield and outfield practice is universally referred to as in and out, or I/O. The outfielders throw to each base during the outfield portion of I/O. Andrew was playing centerfield in the scrimmage and after he made his last throw he sprinted to the bullpen, hurriedly put on his catching gear, and replaced the catcher that was warming up the starting pitcher. I had never seen a player do this during I/O and made a mental note. Andrew later told me he always warmed up pitchers in the bullpen before games, even when he wasn't scheduled to catch, because it enabled him to continue learning the pitching staff. Bullpen catchers bitch frequently because of their thankless job description, and they have to be prodded to perform their duty; yet, the best player on the field was eager to catch in the bullpen completely unsolicited by his coaches. That's impressive, but not as impressive as my initial face-to-face meeting with Andrew. I stopped him as he was leaving the field to introduce myself. We began chatting, and then he excused himself to say goodbye to his family. He hugged his Mom, Dad, grandparents, and girlfriend before rejoining me to finish our conversation. Andrew checked all the boxes: he was an unselfish teammate, he valued his family, and he had Major League power. It definitely seemed too good to be true that he would sign with the Cougars.

After a brief recruiting process Andrew signed with CC, foregoing other NAIA schools because he wanted to be near his family, and the Legend of Warner was underway. His junior season was one for the ages; he hit .478 with 17 home runs and 69 RBI in 51 games culminating with him being named a First Team All-American. Opponents took notice and intentionally walked him TWENTY-FOUR times, which is the equivalent of five or six games that he didn't get an opportunity to swing the bat. There are many amazing Andrew Warner stories, but my favorite took place during his epic junior season. There were ten other teams in our conference, and we played each of the ten schools in a three-game series. Andrew homered AND was intentionally walked vs. EVERY conference opponent. There is no statistical data kept for this incredible feat, but I would wager that no other player in the history of college baseball (all levels) has pulled off this insane double dip! On more than one occasion opposing players asked him to autograph baseballs after he took pre-game BP. Andrew inexplicably did not get drafted upon completion of his junior season. Instead of pouting, his senior season served as an encore for another virtuoso performance that earned him First Team All-American honors for the second consecutive season. The St. Louis Cardinals drafted him in the 40th, and final, round of the 2018 MLB draft. He proved many scouts wrong by earning the MVP of the Florida Gulf Coast League his first minor league season and becoming an All-Star in the New York-Penn League his second minor league season. Andrew's professional career is currently in limbo due to COVID-19, but his legacy as a Columbia College Cougar reigns eternal. Cheers to Baseball and Andrew Warner!

Piper, Wall, and Warner are all even better people than players, and they were just three of forty names that eventually were scrawled on the dry erase board in my office. The greatest challenge with forty newcomers is they hear the team expectations at the first team meeting, but nobody has experienced HOW the program operates on a daily basis. Teaching the HOW for every program detail is crucial to ultimately maximizing success on and off the field. Established winning programs rely heavily on their returners' veteran leadership to indoctrinate newcomers. Our first fall practice in year one featured a bunch of wide-eyed players being talked through the entire practice, from the pre-practice stretch to the post-practice huddle. Year four looked completely different. Veteran players led the practice, and coaches were less involved because expectations were clearly understood. Seeing our team become a cohesive unit was fascinating to watch. After experiencing three rebuilding projects, and building CC Baseball, I prefer building instead of rebuilding. Rebuilding a program requires changing the culture, and eliminating negative players. When building a program, you recruit the entire team, and start with a positive culture day one of year one. Besides, there is nothing better than a honeymoon period!

I personally experienced the royal treatment during my own honeymoon spent on Maui. The mere mention of the word "honeymoon" usually led to a discounted tab or at the very least a complimentary Mai Tai. Most Maui visitors return to the Mainland with memories of picturesque sunsets, seashells, and peaceful ocean breezes. Those traditional island treasures were awesome, but three of my greatest memories from my honeymoon were talking hitting with Paul Molitor, shooting hoops with a topless man, and a brick sidewalk. Paul Molitor is one of the greatest hitters to ever step into the batter's box, and possibly the most underrated player in the history of Major League Baseball. I recognized Paul while we were both waiting outside a souvenir store for our wives to finish shopping, and couldn't pass up an opportunity to talk hitting with an all-time great. "Hey Paul, it was a joy watching you play and congrats on back to back titles with the Blue Jays in '92 and '93. I'm a college baseball coach. Do you mind chatting for a moment?" He was stunned that somebody recognized him on Maui, and also thrilled to take a break from paradise and talk baseball for a half hour. Almost all successful hitters trigger their hands slightly backwards, before going forwards, as the pitch is approaching the hitting zone. Paul Molitor is a rare exception to this universal hitting fundamental, and amassed 3,319 hits in his Hall of Fame MLB career while his hands hit from a dead stop. I asked him about his unorthodox approach to hitting a baseball, and his answer has remained a powerful coaching lesson my entire career, "I guess if somebody is good at something don't change what they are doing." His message provided a simple concept, yet was acutely profound. Paul Molitor was soft-spoken, humble, gracious with his time to a complete stranger, and unknowingly shared a lasting piece of coaching advice that I adopted and will always follow. Cheers to Baseball and Paul Molitor!

Enjoying life is greater than any dollar ever earned. I

was walking the beach and stumbled upon a basketball court that overlooked the ocean. An elderly gentleman that I would guess to be in his 70s, and clad in only shorts and tennis shoes, was shooting baskets by himself, and knocking down one set shot after another with a smile on his face. Father Time eventually transforms a hoopster's jump shot into a set shot! I began rebounding for him and struck up a conversation. This topless gentleman was a Boston native that had vacationed on Maui seven years previous, flew back to Boston to gather some belongings, and then returned to Maui permanently. He informed me he was tired of winter, Maui made him happy, and he had not worn a shirt in SEVEN YEARS! Some may find this to be bizarre behavior, but I love it! Can you imagine not wearing a shirt for seven years? I still use this chance encounter with my man in Maui as a lesson for my players to value happiness and don't sweat the small stuff.

You are probably curious how a brick sidewalk is relevant, or of remote interest, when visiting Maui. The following story is a complete sidebar, but is my all-time 'small world' moment in life. My hometown of Mexico, MO was known as the firebrick capital of the world. I spent my college summers working the graveyard shift at National Refractories, which was one of the brick factories in Mexico. During our honeymoon, I was sitting on a bench sipping a Mai Tai, and waiting for Sarah to complete another shopping spree. Upon glancing down at the brick sidewalk I noticed each brick was stamped, "National Refractories Mexico, MO." There was a chance, albeit a remote chance, that I made those bricks. I dare you to top my small world moment!

My honeymoon was memorable and so was the first

year for CC Baseball. Everybody loves a brand new team much like everybody loves the backup quarterback; because they haven't played a game, which means they haven't LOST a game! The local media coverage of Columbia College Baseball's first team was unparalleled to anything I had ever seen for a small college baseball program. Anne Rogers was a senior journalism student at the University of Missouri and was assigned to cover our program. She was incredible! Our players and coaches were interviewed after every home game. Anne's thorough coverage made a small college baseball team playing at a city park feel like big leaguers. An example of her dedication was exhibited during a conference doubleheader. The second game played slower than molasses, and Mother Nature frowned on us with strong winds and temperatures in the 40s. We finished the second game just shy of midnight and Anne was frozen solid waiting outside the dugout, bundled in winter gear, to interview me and our stars of the game. I am not surprised that only three years after covering CC Baseball she fast-tracked to become a full-time beat writer for the Kansas City Royals. I'm honored that Anne wrote the foreword for my book. Cheers to Baseball and Anne Rogers!

o o o o o oo

Rain created havoc with our schedule and caused us to play our final six conference games in six days to conclude our honeymoon season. We improbably won all six games to become conference co-champions. In four seasons of existence, I'm proud that Cougars Baseball has numerous achievements including a graduation rate in the 90<sup>th</sup> percentile, two conference championships, and two national tournament appearances. However, the players on our first team, that had the courage and belief to join a non-existent program, will always have a special place in Cougar lore. Personally, seeing a homeless program evolve into a dog pile after our final regular-season game was a helluva ride that I will never forget!

# Chapter Five:
# Great People = Great Results

In the introduction, I advised that my keys to leadership were not the gospel. Sorry to contradict myself, but I treat the following as gospel: **Surround yourself with great people to achieve great results.** This simple concept has been the most instrumental leadership technique I've utilized to obtain success in coaching and in life. "Great" might be the most improperly overused word in the English language, and it frequently serves more like hyperbole than earned description. The people you surround yourself with only fall under the "great" category if they are completely trustworthy. I attended a leadership conference early in my career and the speaker said something that has stuck with me forever, "You bring three things with you every day; your knowledge, your attitude, and your people." Take a minute, and rank the three aforementioned attributes in order of importance, before reading any further. This may be a compelling and thought-provoking exercise for some, but my order is simple; people are the runaway winner, attitude is a distant second, and knowledge is a distant third. Choosing great people in every facet of your operation enhances your ability to succeed as a leader. People that directly impact our baseball program are assistant coaches, players, and my inner circle. I have been blessed to have many great assistant coaches, but the one constant is Craig "Boomer" McAndrews.

A college baseball coach spends as much time with his coaching staff as his own family. One of my personal objectives is to have an enjoyable existence with my assistant coaches. I've never understood, regardless of win/loss results, coaching staffs that have an acrimonious relationship. My 20th wedding anniversary is New Year's Eve, 2020. Boomer and I are beginning our 15th anniversary coaching together in 2020, and that doesn't include our one-year player/coach relationship. I promise you I have spent as much time with Boomer as Sarah Munns over the past 15 years! When I recruited Boomer (the player) my instincts told me he had innate leadership qualities, but I could have never predicted he would become my long-time assistant coach. When hiring an assistant coach I use the following "Big 3" checklist:

* Loyal and trustworthy: I value these qualities ahead of knowledge and coaching expertise. Another program can have the smartest pitching coach, hitting coach, or shrewdest recruiter if that person can't be trusted. Just as Don Maines taught me the game, and how to recruit, I'm happy to teach a young assistant. I'm a big believer if you show up on time and try, you will be successful in life.

* Passion for the game: Many players love being a baseball player instead of loving to play baseball; likewise, many coaches love to be a baseball coach instead of loving to coach baseball. These statements are not just a cute play on words, but the absolute truth.

* Mature enough to socially disconnect from the players/students: Two impermissible acts will get you terminated as a college coach. This terrible twosome is exceeding your budget and fraternizing with players or students. Young coaches have a choice between risking their career or partying with their players.

In addition to acing the "Big 3" on a daily basis for fifteen years, I discovered early in Boomer's first season that he excelled at throwing batting practice. Baseball differentiates itself from other sports by requiring coaches to physically enable practice sessions by hitting a fungo and throwing BP. The art of throwing BP is attempted by many, but it is mastered by few. BP is how hitters hone their craft, and the person feeding the BP is an essential cog in the operation. The best BP pitchers feed endless strikes and serve as a live pitching machine for hitters, akin to world champion dart players continuously sticking darts in the bulls-eye. Boomer feeds perfect BP to our hitters, and is remarkably able to repeat the process every day. His efforts provide a huge advantage to our program because, simply put, our hitters take more quality swings than other programs. We are blessed to have one of the best BP arms in the world. A hitter's development is severely stunted if he is unable to take quality BP. Here is a tip for all amateur coaches: Purchase the best pitching machine your budget allows in lieu of coaches feeding awful BP to your hitters. While a live arm is ideal for BP, a live arm that doesn't throw strikes is counterproductive.

Boomer is far from just a prop for our hitters. He has become one of the best college hitting coaches in the country, is the swing doctor for several professional players, and proof is in the numbers. In recent years college baseball has turned to the advent of using various metrics to measure offensive success, and highly sophisticated video equipment as tools for hitters. My measurement is very simple and the essence of winning a baseball game; RUNS PER GAME! Boomer has guided our offense for fifteen seasons, and we have averaged over six runs per game in fourteen of those seasons. You give yourself a really good chance to win games averaging over six runs per game. I'm also a believer you get better hitting a baseball by……. hitting a baseball. My all-time favorite player, Pete Rose, validated our hitting philosophy when I had a chance to talk hitting with him. My wife surprised me for my 40th birthday by throwing a party in Las Vegas with thirty of our closest friends. I was strolling through Caesars Palace and saw Pete was hawking his autographed goods at a sports memorabilia store. I bought a $400 package of signed items from Charlie Hustle, but really was purchasing an opportunity to sit down with Baseball's all-time hits leader to talk baseball. As Pete was signing his number 14 jersey for me, I informed him I was a college baseball coach. He was half-interested and continued signing the jersey. At the risk of having my session abruptly ended with my boyhood idol, I made a comment that bought me a half-hour, "You're my all-time favorite player, and I appreciate your hit record of 4,256 career hits, but you should have had 4,257 career hits." Pete snapped his head at me and retorted, "What the fuck's that supposed to mean. I hit a lot of balls hard right at people." I said, "I remember a game at old Busch Stadium when you hit a one hop line drive to Andy Van Slyke in right field with the bases loaded, he threw out Dave Van Gorder at home plate, and it cost you a hit." Charlie Hustle smiled and stated, "You are right. That Van Gorder was a slow mother fucker." I'm not even positive those particular details were completely accurate when recited to Pete, as I was recalling from memory, but he loved the fact that I had a vested interest in his career.

I cherished the time spent with Pete. We sat at a card table equipped with a nine-inch monitor that displayed horse racing. After all, Charlie Hustle had to keep an eye on his four-legged wagers! We talked baseball for thirty minutes and I hung on every word spoken by Baseball's Hit King. He was a rambling fountain of baseball recollection that was pure beauty for a baseball junkie like Yours Truly. I got a kick out of the fact that he was referring to me as "Coach," and even momentarily halted our baseball conversation to tell me, "Coach, you gotta pull for this horse. It's my best play of the day." I had to pinch myself to think I was talking baseball, and better yet, pulling for Pete Rose's preferred pony...with Pete Rose! We talked head first slides, switch hitting, Whitey Herzog, the designated hitter, his Hall of Fame exclusion, Gaylord Perry's spitball, the Big Red Machine, and his best recommendation to becoming a better hitter. What better person to ask about hitting than the man that has accumulated more hits than anybody to ever play the game of baseball. Pete looked me square in the eye and said, "You get better as a hitter by hitting. I promise you I practiced hitting a baseball more than anybody that has ever walked the planet." Who would have thought that Pete Rose and Boomer shared the same hitting philosophy; hit, hit, and hit some more! Boomer is a tremendous hitting coach, but an even better person. Surrounding myself with great people started with hiring Craig "Boomer" McAndrews as my assistant coach, and every one of my accomplishments in the past fifteen seasons would not have been possible without his assistance.

Leaders can have ambitious motives, and employ great assistants, but ultimately your players are what dictate your success. As a college coach, unlike high school coaches, I get to choose who plays in our program. There are two necessary ingredients when I recruit a player. They must be a good person, and they must possess enough talent to play at the college level. I use the recruiting visit as my interview for recruits. The recruit, regardless of ability level, is done being recruited if he disrespects his parents during the visit. He is also done being recruited if he badmouths his former coaches (high school, juco, summer ball, etc.). Any young man that disrespects his parents or badmouths a former coach, will definitely disrespect and badmouth their college coach. The hardest part about my job, without question, is telling amateur players they are not good enough to play for us, and they are not welcome to join our program. Nobody enjoys being told "you are not good enough." Many of today's amateur players only know preferential treatment regarding earning a roster spot or playing time. Parental politics far too often influence a high school coaches' decisions, and writing a big check will usually get a player "selected" for their "select" travel ball team. I tell every recruit that visits, "Guys that perform the best, and work the hardest, earn the playing time. It doesn't matter if you are a freshman or senior, if you receive a scholarship or are a walk-on, and your last name sure as hell doesn't earn you playing time." I firmly believe in the adage, "the hardest people to judge are yourself and your children." Most parents are initially pissed that I tell them Junior is not good enough to play in our program. They should actually thank me for saving them over $100,000 in costs for their golden child over the course of four years.

Every team has three player classifications; leaders, followers, and turds. Obviously, any successful team's foundation is built on strong positive leadership. The neutral harmless followers always tilt toward the majority of the group, so count on them following the leaders' commitment to the program. So, why have any turds? Let me explain the Munns Turd Theory. I profess that to achieve ideal team chemistry, and create a winning culture, your roster has to consist of less than 10% turds. We carry approximately forty players, so two to four is my maximum turd count. We have all waged the frustrating battle vs. a strand of Christmas lights. Turds on a roster are like bulbs on a strand of Christmas lights. A couple of faulty lights can be located and fixed to save the strand of Christmas lights. More than a couple of faulty lights and your holiday décor is destined for the trash. The two-part mandatory caveat for rolling the dice on a turd is they, first, must be superior difference-making talents, before indulging in a high level risk/reward proposition. Secondly, I have to instinctively see the potential for them to improve from turd to follower. A person is capable of shedding their turd-like tendencies if they have been trapped in a negative culture that lacks spelled-out team expectations. The switch to a positive winning culture, and being surrounded by positive leaders, can do wonders. The other key to rehabilitating a turd is having an open, direct, and honest conversation with them during the recruiting process that sounds like this, "I have heard you had some hiccups at your last school. You will have a clean slate in our program. You will be around great people in a winning culture and will have a lot of fun playing baseball. I will dismiss you from the team if you can't buy into how we do things. I believe in you, know you would be a great fit, and would love to have you join our program." I have witnessed incoming turds easily transition to followers, and some even become leaders in our program.

There are two types of leaders; the vocal leader that leads by example, and the quiet leader that leads by example. Both styles are effective methodology, and the critical common denominator is "leads by example." When your best players are also your hardest workers, the organization's odds of achieving optimal success are substantially increased. Michael Jordan, Tom Brady, and Derek Jeter are all-time greats, and their resumes speak for themselves. However, their work ethic and leadership are what differentiate them from other great players. Every team member is held accountable, and their performance is elevated, when your best players lead by example. Great players that are also great leaders are internally motivated, have an unwavering will to be the best, and genuinely care about team success at all times. Integrity is defined as, "the state of being honest and having strong moral principles." I define "athletic integrity" as an athletes' commitment level when nobody else is watching. The three "bilities" are key ingredients for athletic integrity, and a player being a respected leader. The three "bilities" are availability, dependability, and credibility.

I steadfastly maintain that a player's greatest ability is their availability. This simple skill of showing up every single day is becoming a lost art with today's players. The NBA coined the term "load management," as teams rest their healthy superstars to keep them fresh during the season. What a joke! The disabled list in MLB reaches record numbers every season. I don't expect every player to emulate Cal Ripken Jr.'s durability, but I scoff at today's player that can't practice or play when they are not 100%. The words strain, illness, and contusion on an injury list scream SOFT PLAYER! Dependability is earned through consistent behavior. The consistent player is the most dependable player, and this principle applies to work ethic and performance. As a coach, I love knowing what I'm getting from a player every single day in off-season workouts, practices, and games. There are minor league pitchers that have the same equipment (velocity and pitch action) as the elite arms in MLB. The difference between the electric arm in the minors and the front line MLB ace is consistency. The minor leaguer can't repeat performance. Max Scherzer, Gerrit Cole, Adam Wainwright, etc. consistently repeat performance. I define credibility as a **lengthy** body of behavior that gains the **blind** trust of your fellow teammates and coaches. I highlighted "lengthy" and "blind" because those are the factors that determine a person's credibility. A player that does everything right all the time builds credibility. All players are committed in the short term, but the real test is their dedication over the course of time. There are players I **blindly** trust if they call me and say they are going to be a few minutes late to a team function because of an unforeseen circumstance, and other players I have doubts when they make the same call.

That is the essence of credibility. Try this simple exercise to illustrate the importance of credibility: Scroll through your cell phone, assign a level of credibility for each person, and you will appreciate the measurement that is credibility.

I have been blessed to surround myself with players that were great leaders. Two examples occurred while I coached at William Woods that illustrate your best players exhibiting athletic integrity. L.J. Watson joined our program as a Division 1 transfer from St. Louis University, and he was a five-tool player. Professional scouts assign the following five tools to amateur players; foot speed, arm strength, defensive ability, hitting for average, and hitting for power. When a player excels at all five he is deemed "five-tool." L.J. was even greater at the sixth tool, which is leadership. We had lost the conference championship game, and the spring semester was already completed. Our players' lone duty the day after a devastating loss was attending their coach/player exit meeting, before heading home for summer break. Players signed up for their meetings, with the upperclassmen getting first choice for ten-minute time slots between 9 AM and 5 PM. The upperclassmen typically chose the earlier slots so they can flee campus sooner than later. L.J. had just completed his junior year and signed up for the very last time slot. He walked into the office and I told him I was surprised he chose the latest slot. He replied, "I wanted to go last so we can discuss any issues or information that came up during all the other player meetings to help us get ready for next season." Wow! Our best player unselfishly stuck around, after a devastating loss, because he was already eyeing next season. For the record, we won the conference L.J.'s senior season and qualified for the national tournament. After we were eliminated in the national tournament during his senior season, L.J. chose the last coach/player meeting again. I asked L.J., "Why are you going last when you are a senior and won't be back next season?" His reply is the ultimate in leadership, "My career is over, but I want the program to build off our success and continue to get better." Double Wow! A player that has completed his career still signs up for the last meeting because he cares about the future of the program. That, my friends, is leadership with a capital L! To this day, thanks to L.J.'s tutelage, I schedule the leaders in our program to be the final coach/player interviews. Cheers to Baseball and L.J. Watson!

Jacob Harrison was a local product that signed with William Woods on a partial scholarship. He had slightly above average ability, but his tireless work ethic and fierce competitiveness elevated him to becoming a great player. His Dad, Dan Harrison, builds swimming pools for a living and is the **only** parent in my coaching career that made this suggestion after we signed Jacob, "If Jacob doesn't work hard enough....take away his scholarship." Cheers to Baseball and Dan Harrison! We were hosting a summer tournament for high school travel ball teams. The first game of the tournament was at 8 AM. Our Graduate Assistant Coach, Andy Hight, called me the night before and said, "Hey, just so you know, Harrison is meeting me at 7 AM for his infield workout before the first game of the tournament." Andy applies to the "surround yourself with great people" doctrine. His Dad was one of my high school baseball coaches, and he was a no-brainer hire that contributed mightily to the success of our program. Cheers to Baseball and Andy Hight! Coach Hight was nearing the end of Jacob's 45-minute meticulous infield workout when the "elite" travel ball teams arrived at 7:40 for their 8:00 first pitch. They lazily trudged into our facility, wearing tailored uniforms (some of which were sloppily untucked), while dragging personalized team bags. They appeared to be on a death march instead of being enthused to play America's Past Time. Both coaches explained that they were "show and go" (baseball term for show up and play without properly warming up) because of the early start time. I welcomed the coaches as Coach Hight continued to pepper Jacob with endless ground balls.

The travel ball coaches immediately broke into a conversation/pissing contest debating which of their teams had the most D1 level players. This travel ball ritual is commonplace for summer skippers that merely measure a player by the fourth letter in the alphabet and the first digit in the common counting progression. I asked what they thought of the player working out, since the two assclowns in my presence were oblivious to Jacob providing them a live instructional video on infield play. Both were in awe of Jacob's ability, physical stamina, and work ethic. One of the coaches asked, "Is he a Mizzou guy or local pro guy?" I could not resist providing a truthful answer that also proved a point, "No, he plays for us at William Woods and he is one of the best defenders in the country. He's successful because he is dedicated to his craft, and he doesn't give a damn about uniforms and travel bags. He arrived at 6:30 to properly warm up before his 45-minute infield workout. He will be done shortly because he works every day helping his Dad build swimming pools." I was in all my glory witnessing an old-school throwback player like Jacob Harrison on full display for our guests. Jacob completed his infield workout, **sprinted** off the field, thanked Coach Hight, and hustled from the facility so he wasn't late for an all-day date with manual labor. Cheers to Baseball and Jacob Harrison!

The third piece in the "Surround Yourself with Great People" equation is your inner circle of confidants relative to your occupation. Your inner circle should inform you when your fly is unzipped or a booger is dangling from your nostril. However, there is a helluva lot more to joining my inner circle than zippers and boogers! Everybody has a Triple F Club – friends, family, and fools. While my Triple F Club is full of fun people, only a few of them meet all the criteria for my inner circle. I apply the following four rules when choosing my inner circle:

* Inner circle must be 100% loyal and trustworthy: This sounds familiar because it's also the number one quality I covet when hiring an assistant coach. Your inner circle is built on trust. You need to ask yourself if your inner circle's members genuinely have your best interest at heart and if they are capable of confidentiality. Many good people fail at the latter.

* Choose inner circle members outside of your organization: I trust Boomer with my life, let alone my baseball life, but using an unbiased outsider lends added perspective. I have gained helpful information, throughout my career, from my inner circle. Team chemistry issues, disciplinary decisions, and game strategy are examples of program topics that I have bounced off my inner circle.

* Your inner circle needs to have walked in your shoes: I'm seeking problem-solving advice applicable to leading a college baseball program from my inner circle. Therefore, my inner circle consists of college baseball coaches, former college baseball coaches, or those connected to college baseball because they are an educated voice that has dealt with the same situations in the same occupation.

* Keep a **SMALL** inner circle: Sadly, I have seen multiple coaching friends unjustly terminated, or forced to resign, because their inner circle grew too large and a member stabbed them in the back. Wisely choose your inner circle! Your inner circle is designed to assist with important organizational issues, and is not a survey for the masses. I recommend two to four people to serve as your inner circle.

**You never know** how your closest friendships will be formed in life, and who will eventually comprise your inner circle. Joaquin Andujar pitched for the St. Louis Cardinals in the 80s, was a fan favorite, and won game seven of the 1982 World Series for the Redbirds. Joaquin was a Dominican Republic native learning the English language on the fly, and when he was asked his favorite word, he replied, "**youneverknow**." The man nicknamed "One Tough Dominican" had no idea he had perfectly, and prophetically, wrapped three words into one. Early in my Drexel career, I befriended Mike Morhardt (better known as Mo), who was an assistant coach for our conference foe, the University of Hartford. I was offered an opportunity to run summer baseball camps in New Brunswick, Canada. I invited Mo to join me for this excursion into the unknown, and he immediately accepted my invitation. I quickly discovered during our nightly sessions talking baseball, while consuming Alpine lagers, that Mo was a baseball savant. This should have come as no surprise, considering his lineage. Mo was a two-sport college athlete, having played baseball and basketball at the University of Hartford. His uncle, Moe Morhardt, played in the big leagues for the Chicago Cubs, and was a college baseball coach. His cousin, Greg Morhardt, was formerly a scout for the Anaheim Angels and was instrumental in signing Mike Trout. Mo no longer coaches college baseball, but has remained connected to athletics his entire adult life by coaching high school sports, AAU girls basketball, and serving as a clinician and individual instructor for WINS For Life. More importantly, he cares about people and has positively impacted countless youngsters. He truly "gets it" and I'm grateful to utilize him as a trusted resource in my inner circle. Cheers to Baseball and Mike Morhardt!

I met New Orleans native, Omar Jefferson, in the Athletic Training room at Drexel University. He was getting his master's degree from Temple University, and he was assigned to the Drexel Athletic Department to accumulate practical hours required for his degree. Omar is an incredible Athletic Trainer, the king of the craps table, a walking fountain of sports information, and most importantly a member of my inner circle. It's crazy to think that a lifelong bond between a part-time baseball coach from mid-Missouri and a student trainer from The Big Easy was born in downtown Philly. 100% trustworthy is the first criteria for inclusion into my inner circle. I have trusted Omar to be the godfather of my only child, so I sure as hell trust his feedback pertinent to running a college baseball program. Cheers to Baseball and Omar Jefferson!

○ ○ ○ ○ ○ ○ ○ ○

The hit game show, *Who Wants to Be a Millionaire,* debuted in 1999 and is still running 22 seasons later. Contestants attempt to win the grand prize of one million dollars by answering a series of trivia questions that increase in difficulty level. A popular feature on the show was contestants being afforded a "lifeline," and allowed to phone a friend for assistance when they were stumped by a question. I strongly advise creating an inner circle so you can phone a friend when necessary. Who would have thought that two lifelines in my inner circle result-ed from a blind date to Eastern Canada, and a chance meeting in an Athletic Training room. As Joaquin said, "youneverknow!"

# Chapter Six:
# Fun, Fun, and More Fun

Why is "fun" not a priority for organizations, especially college athletic teams which are comprised of athletes that began playing their sport as a kid because they had fun? My lead agenda item in our first team meeting, after welcoming our players back to campus and introducing our assistant coaches, is emphasizing that we will have structure, have discipline, and have FUN. "Nice job" is a common coach compliment directed at players in youth, high school, and college athletics. I prefer "atta boy," "great play," and "now we're having fun" as superlatives for players, to avoid even the subliminal message that playing baseball is a job. Bill Belichick's famous order for New England Patriot players is, "do your job!" NFL players are employees and it is indeed their job to play professional football, but amateur athletes should be playing for the love of the game. I once taught an undergraduate Sports Psychology course for aspiring high school and college coaches while at William Woods. While I chose the PE General degree instead of teaching as a college undergraduate, I got a thrill out of mentoring soon-to-be coaches. The students in the class were either college athletes or former high school athletes. My favorite exercise was asking each student to make a list of their ten most important characteristics for the team they will coach, and rank their characteristics from 1-10 with one being the most important. I also made a list. I would challenge the class of 15-20 students that none of them would include my number one trait on their list. The order of importance varied, but lists contained the usual traits, such as work ethic, accountability, unselfishness, loyalty, toughness, etc. All of these and others are worthy of being listed, but fun rarely made a single list. After all of the students' lists had been collected and revealed, I would ask these questions to stimulate conversation and debate:

1) Did you perform better in practice and games if you were having **fun**?

2) Did your teams collectively perform better in practice and games if they were having **fun**?

3) Have you ever quit a sport you were good at because it was not **fun**?

4) What will you do to make the sport you coach more **fun**?

5) Would you now include **fun** on your top ten list?

6) If so, where do you rank **fun**?

The answer to question five was unanimously "yes," and I am hopeful the exercise made a lasting impression on future coaches to value the importance of fun for their teams. The answer to question six frequently ascended from unranked to number one! Corporate America has bought into the theory that a happy worker is a more productive worker. Successful companies implement employee-friendly strategies such as casual dress instead of business attire, plush office furniture instead of the traditional cubicle, working-from-home has become a more prevalent option (even before the COVID-19 pandemic), and rewarding their employees with cool social gatherings. Google is one of the world's most powerful companies and has taken fun to a new level for their employees. Features include sleep pods for napping, a free cafeteria that serves steak and lobster, and massage rooms...just to name a few. Places of worship have even replaced traditional services with new age strategies to lure more members and make church fun. Padded seats have replaced wooden pews, live modern music has replaced hymn books, shorts and flip flops have replaced stuffy formal clothing, and the church I attend even supplies FREE DONUTS for the congregation. What better way to a person's heart than a free donut! Contrarian changes leading to major positive results are being achieved by two institutional entities, such as Corporate America and churches, yet many coaches fail to inject fun into their program.

Youth sports are the foundation, and the initial feeder programs, for college athletics. The "fun factor" is diminished in youth baseball for two primary reasons; the players' inactivity and the parental pressure when a player fails. There is a reason youth soccer is booming. Youth baseball players stand around like statues the majority of their games, while youth soccer players constantly run up and down the field engaged in the action. Activity equals interest! An even bigger factor that converts youth baseball players to becoming youth soccer players is parental pressure when a player fails. Baseball is a game of failure. The greatest MLB hitters post a .300 batting average, which means they fail 70% of the time. There are not many professions that qualify you as a Hall of Famer with a 30% success rate. A youth baseball player is **under the microscope** to throw strikes as a pitcher, make plays as a defender, and get a hit while batting. For example, a youth baseball player strikes out to end the game with the bases loaded and his team down by one run. The player feels terrible, and far too often parents/youth coaches criticize the player instead of supporting him. That same player blends into the ongoing back and forth for the entirety of his soccer game, and is **NEVER under the microscope**. The only exception might be a goalie that has a ball scoot through his wickets for a game-winning goal. Which of those experiences is more fun for a ten-year-old? This simple equation is your answer; idle time + parental pressure after failure = switch to soccer. This equation can be averted by baseball coaches at all levels.

A sickening baseball practice, far too commonplace from youth baseball to college baseball, consists of a coach or player feeding batting practice while one player hits, and every other player (most of whom are playing out of position in the field or not playing a position at all) lazily shag the balls that are hit. I refer to this drill in futility as BS BP. For example's sake, let's say there are 15 team members. That means one out of 15 players are active in BS BP, and 14 players are inactive. Would a company benefit if one in 15 employees was working to improve the bottom line? Another example of minimizing production is during defensive drill work. A coach hits ground balls to nine infielders. One infielder is active while eight infielders wait in line for their turn. Instead of one line with nine players, a better plan is to form three lines of three, and players take three times as many ground balls. Self-analysis is ongoing and vital to a leader's short-term and long-term success. The most common question I ask myself during practice is, "Are any players completely inactive, and how can I adjust practice to make them active?" BS BP can easily be replaced with BP that incorporates all phases of the game and is perpetual motion. Here's an example of how productive BP looks:

* A coach feeds BP.

* All players that are not hitting play their primary defensive position, and field every ball the hitter puts in play with game-like intensity.

* Hitters are in groups of four. One player hits live BP and takes 5-7 swings, while the other three players in his group form a bunting station behind the on-field batting cage. The four players in the hitting group rotate from hitting to bunting until all players have taken their swings.

* Another group of four players practices base running; working on reads from first base, second base and third base on every ball the hitter puts in play.

Now that we have 15 out of 15 players active instead of one out of 15 players active, let's address the other dilemma; parental pressure on kids when they fail. Simply put, smile and encourage kids when they fail. A parent/coaches' smile and encouragement is more challenging, but also more impactful, during a kid's moments of failure than during a kid's successful moments.

One of my greatest intrinsic rewards is when a player, or former player, tells me during his exit meeting, "that was the most fun team I've ever played on...." The most reliable measurable that validates the "fun level" in your program is retention rate. College athletic programs, and colleges in general, are applauded and scrutinized based on their graduation rates. I value our retention rate more than our graduation rate. A successful retention rate is a precursor for a successful graduation rate. The chronological order from incoming freshman to alumni is recruitment, retention, and graduation. My annual goal for our retention rate is to land in the 90th percentile. Fun is a genuine and natural reaction that cannot be mandated by a leader. Chevy Chase's character, Clark W. Griswold, in *National Lampoon's Vacation,* proved this point during an all-time classic scene when he attempted to mandate fun. Mr. Griswold was driving the family truckster, trapped in close proximity to his wife and two kids, when he finally lost all patience with a vacation gone awry, and delivered the following rant, "Well I'll tell you something. This is no longer a vacation. It's a quest. It's a quest for fun. You're gonna have fun, and I'm gonna have fun. We're all gonna have so much fucking fun we're gonna need plastic surgery to remove our goddamn smiles! You'll be whistling "Zip-A-Dee-Doo-Dah" out of your assholes! I must be crazy!" Don't become a crazed lunatic like the Griswolds' fearless leader in a quest for fun. Create an environment, and structure your program, where your players (or employees) look forward to showing up every day. As stated earlier in the book, if you haven't seen *National Lampoon's Vacation,* that's your own damn fault!

A fear-based dictatorship style of leadership has

thankfully become nearly extinct. There are numerous examples of great players that excelled while having more fun than their peers. NFL legendary quarterback, Brett Favre, joked with the defensive lineman that was attempting to tear his head off, and ran wildly around the field after delivering a touchdown pass like he was playing Pop Warner football. Ken Griffey Jr. displayed his trademark smile as a Gold Glove centerfielder, and smashed 630 career home runs, on his way to the Hall of Fame. Ervin "Magic" Johnson grinned from ear to ear, and dazzled fans with no-look passes, while leading the Los Angeles Lakers to five NBA titles. The Boston Red Sox and Cincinnati Reds 1975 World Series was arguably the best Fall Classic of all time. Game six was an epic instant classic. In game six, Pete Rose came to the plate in the 11th inning and looked at Red Sox future Hall of Fame catcher, Carlton Fisk, and stated, "Man, this is **fun** playing this game, isn't it?" Fisk would famously wave his walk-off home run fair in the 12th inning to force a game seven that the Reds would eventually win. Fisk's game-winning missile clanked off the leftfield foul pole at Fenway Park, which begs to question why baseballs that hit the foul pole are deemed fair? Shouldn't the large yellow metal poles constructed in the corners of baseball stadiums actually be designated as fair poles? Baseball's greatest oxymoron is akin to driving on the parkway and parking on the driveway. Rose and Fisk are recognized as two of the most competitive old-school hard asses (that is an extreme compliment for a baseball player) in the history of Baseball, yet Rose described a pressure-packed World Series moment as **FUN**!

Far too many people don't enjoy their journey in life,

and thus unnecessarily live a miserable existence. One of our founding forefathers, Ben Franklin, summed it up best, "Most men die at 25, but just aren't buried until they're 75." The man whose face adorns the $100 bill proved he not only rocked an all-time great skullet, but was a prophetic genius for living life to the fullest. For those confused, a skullet is a hairstyle in which the hair is bald at the front and on top, but long in the back. I value good times and friendships over material things, my win/loss record, or money. I've never seen a Brinks truck following a hearse! I've attended many funerals and have never heard a person's wealth uttered in a eulogy memorializing the deceased. I had a front-row seat, and I was influenced to make fun a priority by my Dad, Mr. Dale Eisele. He smiled continuously while enjoying life every day all the way to the finish line. I have fond memories of my Dad telling Bob Gibson stories, sharing our love for playing cards, and laughing with just about everybody he encountered. My Dad's hobbies during retirement were golf and fishing. He spent most days either cussing a golf shot or reeling in fish from a local watering hole. His last two days on Earth epitomize my Dad's zest for life. Two days before passing away, he played the best round of golf he's ever played, and even played an extra nine holes because he felt so good. The next day he told the property owner where he was fishing that he "caught one of the best messes of fish he had ever caught." This was quite a statement from an expert fisherman that could hook a lunker from your toilet. He drove home, cleaned his last mess of fish, then laid down on his bed and peacefully went to sleep forever. Ironically, my Dad was 75 years young when he passed away, but unlike most men from

Ben Franklin's quote, he lived a full 75 years. Cheers to Baseball and my Dad!

Springfield, Illinois is best known as Abraham Lincoln's residence before he became president, and as the home of the horseshoe. Everybody is familiar with one of our greatest U.S. presidents that abolished slavery and whose bearded mug is plastered on the $5 bill. While it is unexplainable why Honest Abe didn't include a mustache with his facial hair ensemble, I can explain the horseshoe. Springfield's famous delicacy is constructed from bottom to top as such; a piece of Texas toast, your choice of meat (hamburger, Buffalo chicken, etc.), French fries, and cheese sauce smothering the entire concoction. Health nuts squint at this masterpiece and it should be served in a body bag, but trust me when I inform you the "shoe" is heavenly. Springfield is one of my favorite cities, has a bar on every corner, and it's where I met Steve Torricelli. Coach Tor is a close friend, coaching colleague, a member of my inner circle, and has as much fun as anybody I've met in life, let alone baseball. He has been a role model for all coaches on how to blend fun with discipline while always remaining player-centered. You mention the name "Coach Tor" to anybody he has befriended and a smile will crease their face immediately. A few small examples exhibited by Coach Tor that go a long way include assigning nicknames to all his players, serving as a gracious host by providing opposing teams a BBQ meal after games (win, lose or draw), and running instructional baseball camps over the years for thousands of Springfield youngsters. Cheers to Baseball and Coach Tor!

One of Coach Tor's favorite phrases is "belly laugh" when he finds something extremely amusing. His motto in life is "the more belly laughs the better!" Since this chapter is "Fun, Fun, and More Fun," let me share the Munns seven-tier laugh ladder in descending order with an interpretation for each:

7) Fake smile: that was really dumb

6) Courtesy chuckle: not remotely funny but I'll be polite

5) Genuine chuckle: fairly funny

4) Open mouth laugh: genuinely funny

3) Belly laugh: very funny and borderline incapacitating

2) Liquid out the nose laugh: hilarious and requires several minutes to recover

1) Drum roll, please...Piss your pants laugh: uncontrollable, ceases your ability to speak, prompts eye-wiping tears, can drop you to the fetal position, and requires a change of underwear

Can you visualize yourself experiencing each of the seven? Do you have other laugh levels you would include in your laugh ladder? Unfortunately, a life-altering event is necessary before some coaches prioritize people and good times ahead of the profession. This may include the death of a loved one, personal illness, or the birth of their child. I have heard countless coaches claim, "My priorities changed and I became a better coach after....." Laugh levels one through three in my tier are priceless and impossible to consistently achieve, but hopefully, this chapter allows you to avoid sweating the small stuff, and not require a life-altering event to enjoy your journey.

Jim Valvano gave one of the most inspirational speeches of all time while accepting the Arthur Ashe Courage and Humanitarian Award at the Espy Awards in 1993. Jimmy V was suffering from cancer and was so frail he relied on the podium to remain upright. He would pass away less than two months after his "Don't Give Up" speech. The first time I heard Jimmy V's legendary speech was while I was lounging in a hotel room in Durham, North Carolina while on a road trip to play Duke University. I cried hearing a man with only weeks to live deliver a powerful and courageous message. I have listened to the same legendary speech hundreds of times since that evening, and have shed a tear every single time I hear his speech. For my money, Jimmy V's message is sage advice for all of us as we navigate life. My personal highlight of his speech was his daily recommendation for mankind, "To me, there are three things everyone should do every day. Number one is **laugh**. Number two is think – spend some time in thought. Number three, you should have your emotions move you to tears. If you **laugh,** think, and cry, that's a heck of a day." I have highlighted the word laugh because although Jimmy V didn't specify a seven-tier laugh ladder, he made laughing a top three priority. Jimmy V spent years dedicating himself to becoming an extremely successful college basketball coach and won an improbable national title at North Carolina State in 1983, but what he did for just over ten minutes at the Espy Awards trumped a lifetime of coaching achievements. He has raised hundreds of millions of dollars posthumously for cancer research thanks to his speech and reminded us all we need to laugh every day. I'm hopeful Google, Coach Tor, my

Dad, the Munns seven-tier laugh ladder, Jimmy V's speech, and even Clark W. Griswold's rant have inspired you to re-evaluate the importance of **FUN**. Yesterday's gone, tomorrow's never promised, so enjoy the Hell out of today!

# Chapter Seven:
# The Dreaded Babbling Chucklehead

The ability to communicate in athletics, and in life, is an essential skill that single-handedly creates transparent relationships, and solves problems before they become problems. We all know a babbling chucklehead that talks a mile a minute and says nothing. More words don't make a great communicator, the choice of words and their timing is what matters. The babbling chucklehead is a headache-waiting-to-happen for their listener, and about as productive as entering a stationary bicycle in the Tour de France. Lance Armstrong, in his prime, could pedal his ass off on a stationary bicycle but would obviously finish dead last. The most knowledgeable person in the world is also completely worthless if he, or she, cannot impart their wisdom on others. I have known coaches that are baseball geniuses but struggle to communicate the game to their players. I have also known coaches that possess average baseball acumen but are phenomenal communicators. The master communicator who lacks knowledge is the preferred choice to lead a team. I even give a dunce a probable chance to succeed if they surround themselves with great people, are masterful communicators, and can motivate their team. A leader that is knowledgeable and is a great communicator has a chance to be special. The listener in communication is 50% of the equation. A leader must identify their listener's comprehension ability which ranges from attentively hanging on your every word to a condition I have classified as "open mouth syndrome." Pay attention the next time you speak to someone and they listen to your words with their mouth wide open. That person usually struggles to comprehend a message and requires extra explanation.

I promise you children, employees, and players HEAR the words spoken by their parents, bosses, and coaches. They not only hear the words, but they LISTEN to the words. There is a vast difference between hearing and listening. Hearing is defined as, "perceive with the ear a sound made." Listening is defined as, "giving one's attention to a sound." The key word that differentiates "hear" and "listen" is ATTENTION. My six-year-old child (Mary Ellen) and numerous players throughout my career have proved this theory. I have made comments to Mary Ellen, and players, that I thought were inconsequential at the time, only to later learn my "inconsequential" comments were recalled as memorable or impactful. Mary Ellen and I were playing at the park when she accidentally knocked another little girl to the ground while waiting to go down the slide. I asked her to help the little girl up because that's the "right thing to do." Fast forward approximately one year; I was picking Mary Ellen up from her daycare facility and her teacher pulled me aside. She told me Mary Ellen had seen Classmate A accidentally knock down Classmate B, and Mary Ellen instructed Classmate A to help up Classmate B because "my Daddy says that's the right thing to do." We had not discussed the original incident, and I did not recall a similar incident taking place in the past year, but my daughter remembered my words. I don't claim to be a perfect parent, and often wonder if I know what the hell I'm doing raising my only child, but that was a Proud Papa moment for sure! Former players have shared personal player/coach memorable verbal exchanges at alumni events or wedding receptions....that I don't even remember! A leader's compliments, advice, constructive criticism, jokes, smart-ass comments, and harsh words all resonate with their recipient.

Miscommunication is the only type of communication worse than poor communication. The word assume has popularly been broken down as a comedic play on letters; ASS U ME. You have probably heard the saying, "when you assume, you make an ASS out of U and ME." There is ample truth in this saying, and the person communicating must be perfectly clear to their listener. Tug McGraw was a successful left-handed pitcher that carved out a twenty-year MLB career, including recording the final out of the 1980 World Series to secure the Philadelphia Phillies their first title in 97 seasons. When Tug was asked if he preferred grass or Astroturf, the zany lefty replied, "I don't know. I never smoked any Astroturf." The Canadian Football League proved to be masters of miscommunication on draft day. Darrell Robertson was taken by the Ottawa Rough Riders in the fourth round of the CFL's dispersal draft in April 1995. Unfortunately for the Rough Riders, Mr. Robertson had tragically died in a car crash on December 5th, 1994. Later in the same year, the Montreal Alouettes selected James Eggnick in the fifth round of the

March 1996 CFL Draft. The problem was Mr. Eggnick had sadly died from cancer the previous December. Two organizations in the Canadian Football League went above and beyond in miscommunication demonstration by drafting two deceased players in a calendar year. They each drafted a corpse! A draftnik is a person obsessed with studying professional sports drafts. Even famous NFL rival draftniks, Mel Kiper Jr. and Todd McShay, would jointly agree that drafting a corpse is a losing proposition for building your football team. RIP Mr. Robertson and RIP Mr. Eggnick!

My favorite case of miscommunication happened on an episode of *The Newlywed Game,* a popular TV game show that debuted in 1966 and ran for over 30 years. Bob Eubanks hosted the show, which featured newly married couples that were asked revealing, often sexually con-notative, questions to determine how well the newlyweds knew each other. During one particular taped episode Eubanks posed this question to a female contestant named Olga, "Where's the most unusual place you've ever made whoopee?" Whoopee was 70s slang for having sex. Even though Mr. Eubanks was requesting a location such as the kitchen floor, while riding on an airplane to join the Mile High Club, your neighbor's front yard, etc.; Olga proclaimed, "That'd be in the ass, Bob." This moment is game show legend, lives in infamous eternal embarrass-ment for Olga, and is a classic example of miscommunica-tion. Needless to say, communication is the lifeline for successful organizations, and miscommunication is an extreme detriment to becoming a successful organization. Don't ASSUME anything!

The first step in communication for a leader is

creating, outlining, and thoroughly reviewing their organization's expectations with all members of their organization. There is a substantial difference between rules and expectations. The very first team meeting, every single year, I review team expectations with all team members (assistant coaches, student managers, players). Team members cannot be held accountable if they don't know what is expected of them in our program. Any organization that does not outline expectations for their members is performing a major disservice. The organization's members are asked to operate in the dark without knowing the building blocks that are essential to carry out a desired mission. How can a successful outcome be obtained if nobody knows the expectations? How can I correct, question, or punish player behavior if they don't know what's expected of themselves? It's easy to correct player behavior during an individual meeting when you can refer to team expectations that were discussed, and distributed, on day one. However, criticizing a player when team expectations are non-existent is completely unfair to that player. The worst feedback that illustrates a serious shortcoming is if a player says to a coach, "I didn't know we did it that way....." I spend considerable time in deep thought while creating team expectations, especially early in my career when initially creating my list. Team expectations are continuously self-analyzed, and sometimes tweaked, for the betterment of the program. My team expectations are what I prioritize as important. Expectations that are valuable to me may not be valuable to you, and vice versa. Regardless of your team expectations, they should be your initial communication to your team and they are absolutely necessary to lead a successful organization. Here are our team expectations:

1) Show respect any time the United States National Anthem is playing.

2) Always be on time or early to all team functions.

3) Be respectful of all people on the Columbia College campus.

4) Be respectful of all service people while representing Columbia College.

5) Pay attention and don't yawn while a teammate or coach is speaking.

6) Never show up a teammate or coach.

7) Never use a negative tone toward a teammate or coach.

8) Do not ask about personal statistics or ever look at the scorebook during a game.

9) No negative connotation toward an umpire.

10) No negative connotation toward an opponent.

11) Never use profanity that would embarrass the program.

12) Never throw equipment.

13) Run hard on every ground ball and fly ball you hit.

14) Run out the outs.

15) Sprint on and off the field unless you are a pitcher.

As mentioned earlier, a leader's words carry influential clout. An identical verbal message, using the same exact words, can be delivered by a coach, but the tone and voice inflection dictate the message. As importantly, a leader's actions, body language, and tone are crucial ingredients for inspiring their team. I expect to be held to a higher standard as a leader and relish that expectation. For example, one of our team expectations is "no negative connotation toward an umpire" (see expectation number nine). It would be hypocritical if I created that expectation and then was consistently ejected from games for arguing with umpires. One of my proudest accomplishments as a head coach is never being ejected from a game during my eighteen-year head coaching career, and never having a player ejected from a game. A player once questioned why I never got ejected because he foolishly rationalized it "would fire the team up." I explained to the player that I value sportsmanship, and believe negative attention toward umpires is a distraction that stunts a player's ability to perform at optimal level. Stan 'The Man' Musial composed a decorated Hall of Fame career that included the following accomplishments: 24-time All-Star, three-time World Series champion, three-time National League MVP, seven-time batting champion, amongst many other worthy achievements. Perhaps his most remarkable achievement was **NEVER** being ejected from a game during his entire career. Stanley Frank Musial should be a sportsmanship reference for all players and coaches. The gigantic statue of Stan The Man that greets fans entering Busch Stadium displays a quote from former MLB Commissioner Ford Frick that sums up The Man: "Here stands baseball's perfect warrior. Here stands baseball's perfect knight."

Body language ALWAYS speaks. As a leader, I cannot display negative body language, especially during difficult times. The greatest teams in the country mix in several "clunkers" during the course of a season, and a leader must maintain positive body language during the "clunkers." Exhibiting poise and positive body language is a tremendous challenge for coaches, but it will resonate with players for both short-term and long-term success. I have suffered excruciating losses as a head coach in high magnitude games, including post-season elimination games and championship games. All eyes are on you as a leader, and the trickle-down reaction from your body language makes a lasting impression on the team. We preach positive body language, and a player will hear, "better body language" from a coach or team leader if improvement is necessary. An example of practicing good body language for players is expectation number 14, "run out the outs." After a player makes an out (ground out, pop out, or fly out) they are expected to jog off the field with their head up instead of walking from the foul line to the dugout with slouched shoulders and their head down. The first description is a player sending a message that he is confident despite his short-term failure, and he cannot be broken. The second description is a walking billboard for defeatist attitude, and commonplace at all levels.

Another in-game version of positive body language is demanding our players give a "hard 90." A "hard 90" is a hitter sprinting through first base on any ground ball they hit to an infielder. The distance from home plate to first base is 90 feet, thus the term "hard 90." I explain to our hitters that a "hard 90" may not make you safe on that particular ground ball, but it sends a message to your opponent that we run out every ground ball. By executing expectation number 13, your opponent's infielders observe that they must hurry defensively, and their hurried play increases the probability that an error will occur on a similar ground ball hit later in the same game. A player's routine ground out while giving a "hard 90" in the fourth inning could be a prerequisite for a rally-starting error in the ninth inning. Most players sprint from home to first base in approximately four seconds. In essence, our players are being asked to sprint for 16 seconds if they ground out four times. I don't think 16 seconds of effort is too much to ask. Another incentive is our players get an instant ticket to sit the bench the rest of the game if they fail to give a "hard 90." Playing time is the ultimate trump card for a coach! A similar example happens frequently in basketball. A player finishes a fast break with a resounding dunk and sprints back to play defense with a bounce in his step. The same player misses a layup or easy shot at the end of a fast break, and he runs half speed with his head down to get back on defense. Motivating an athlete to hustle and display positive body language, when they fail, is one of the greatest challenges as a coach!

An entire book could be written on baseball communication. I have chosen two communication systems that top my chronological list of importance, and are absolutely necessary to safely and efficiently operate as a unit. We implement these communication systems before our players ever step on the field. Pitcher/catcher communication initiates the action in baseball much like the center/quarterback exchange in football. The catcher flashes numerical signs in his crotch area, while in a squatted position, to signify which pitch he prefers from the hurler's repertoire. The pitcher can shake off the catcher's suggestion and choose another pitch, but the pitcher and catcher (known in baseball lingo as "the battery") must arrive at a unified pitch selection. Another component of the strategic equation is to disguise which pitch will be thrown to insure the opponent does not steal the catcher's signs. The Houston Astros cheated their way to winning the 2019 World Series by designing an elaborate system to steal opposing catcher's signs, and relay the oncoming pitch to their hitters. Catchers with "smart fingers" have a better chance to get hitters out, but they also need to know which pitch is being thrown for their personal well-being. Being "crossed up" is a nightmarish, and potentially unsafe, experience for catchers. For example, a catcher is anticipating a breaking ball from the pitcher, and he receives a fastball instead. This miscommunication becomes a 100 mile per hour game of dodge ball for the catcher, and usually elicits the pitcher getting his ass chewed out during a mound visit.

Pop up/fly ball communication and prioritization is a necessity in order for players to collectively function in a game setting. Our program uses "ball, ball, ball" as the verbal command from a player that wants to catch a pop up or fly ball that is in flight. Any defenders that are in close proximity to the player reply, "you, you, you." This simple exchange allows multiple players to operate fearlessly on balls in the air. What if multiple players are calling, "ball, ball, ball?" That's when prioritization is utilized. Our pop up/fly ball priority list is as follows: centerfielder, corner outfielders, shortstop, second base-man, third baseman, first baseman, catcher, and the pitcher is the last resort. For example, if the centerfielder, shortstop, and second baseman are all calling for a shallow fly ball behind second base, the centerfielder has priority because he is ahead of the other two positions on our priority list. Multiple players traveling full speed, with eyes in the sky, need the aforementioned communication and prioritization to avoid violent collisions. Pitcher/catcher and pop up/fly ball communication systems exist in every MLB organization and every good college program. The key to a successful system is all players using consistent terminology, and completely understanding their team's mode of operation.

Umpire communication is overlooked and undervalued by players and coaches. Three human elements influence 100% of our games; players, coaches, and umpires. Yet, many folks that pull on baseball pajamas struggle with umpire communication, especially when debating a call. This has become a lost art in the big leagues thanks to instant replay recently being incorporated. In past years fans were treated to some classic skipper/umpire rhubarbs. Longtime Atlanta Braves manager Bobby Cox, sprayed umpires with tobacco juice for years, and holds the MLB record for ejections (162). John McGraw is a distant second on this dubious leader board with 121. While past MLB skippers have provided comedic theatre for fans, their antics rarely overturned a call. Billy Martin kicked dirt on umpires, Earl Weaver turned his cap backwards to get nose-to-nose with the men in blue, and Lou Piniella pried bases from the ground and heaved them across the infield. I was not privy to Billy the Kid, the Earl of Baltimore, or Sweet Lou's commentary while they behaved as petulant children, but here are a couple of personal favorites I have heard; directed at the home plate umpire calling balls and strikes, "turn around, bend over, and use your good eye" and after a coach asked an umpire to smile, "I always knew assholes had teeth!" These two insulting remarks are sure to get you instantly dumped, but they don't serve as Baseball's universal word for an automatic ejection.

*Bull Durham* was a 1988 movie classic, and pure cinematic genius that depicted life in the minor leagues. Kevin Costner's character, Crash Davis, played a leading role as the Durham Bulls catcher. There were a plethora of memorable scenes in *Bull Durham* that are repeated verbatim for baseball players, baseball coaches, sports fans, and anybody that appreciates good humor. The funniest scene, in a film full of funny scenes, might be Crash Davis arguing a close play at the plate after a runner had been called safe. Crash began by stating it was a cocksucking call, and after a lengthy debate breaking down the implications and consequences for using the word cocksucker, Crash was ejected after this final heated exchange:

*Umpire:* "Call me a cocksucker again, and you're outta here.

*Crash:* "You're a cocksucker!"

*Umpire:* "You're outta here!"

Therefore, 1988 became the birth year for the word "cocksucker" serving as THE forbidden expletive when addressing an umpire. Lawyers, and those that have been married for a long time, understand the art of winning an argument. I learned early in my career to ask an umpire this open-ended question when questioning a call, "What did you have there?" It is much easier to prove somebody wrong if you don't provide them with the answer in your question. Here is an example of a poor way to initiate umpire communication, "The runner left the baseline. He has to give our player a chance to catch the ball...." I have afforded the umpire plenty of information to form, or concoct, a rebuttal. "What did you have there?" makes the umpire initiate his opinion. One of the greatest baseball trivia questions is a trick question that illustrates this concept of providing the answer in the question. "Who has the most wins and has never won a Cy Young Award?" The answer is Cy Young. They named the award for him long after his career was completed.

Over-communication is a strategy I use to impart the MOST important messages to our players in hopes that those messages are permanently retained. Our pitcher's throwing arms are cherished, and they are the physical lifeblood for us winning games. Therefore, I take every arm precaution throughout our fall season, off-season, pre-season, and in-season. In addition, I ask every one of our pitcher's every single day, "How's your arm feel?" I'm certain my obsession with each of their arms gets annoying for them, but over-communication is warranted for a body part that decides winning and losing. An in-game example of over-communicating occurs with our catchers. The catcher is the field general, and our catchers call their own pitches. Needless to say, they are the engine that drives our defense. When our catcher is hitting and makes the last out of an inning, especially if it's with the bases loaded or with runners in scoring position, I sit next to him while he puts on his catching equipment (also known in baseball lore as the "tools of ignorance"). I wear out his ear reminding him to have a short memory, while emphasizing that we need him locked in calling pitches.

The reply is always a pissed off, "I got it," or "I know." Interpretation: "Get off my ass Coach! You do this every time I make a big out to end an inning." I would rather over-communicate and have our catcher furious with me in the short term than have our catcher dwell on a failed at-bat, and negatively impact his defense. Here are a few other Munnsisms over-communicated because I strongly believe they translate to winning:

* Throw strikes and play defense: Self-explanatory

* Don't play to the score: Maintain the same level of focus and intensity regardless of the score of the game.

* Compete: Emphasize the single-most-important quality to a player during high-leverage situations; competitiveness.

* Have fun and be a great teammate: Usually concludes most pre-game speeches to emphasize two important "controllables," and de-emphasize the pressure of performance.

Another example of over-communicating with our players has nothing to do with the game of baseball, but it has everything to do with the game of life. A regular post-practice or post-game message addresses two social lapses in judgment that can potentially result in fatal endings:

1) Don't drink and drive, and don't let your friends drink and drive.

2) Walk away from confrontation.

I don't preach morality to our team, but I deal with reality. The majority of 18 to 22-year-old college students consume alcohol. My goal is to emphasize they don't get behind the wheel and endanger themselves or others. Number one on my list of two used to be the only item on my list. I added "walk away from confrontation" because of the senseless gun violence that exists in our world. The message driven home to our players is swallow your pride, and take the less macho route by walking away from confrontation. I inform them that they have more at stake than some hooligan baiting them into confrontation. Ultimately players will make their own decisions, but getting ahead of these two potential pitfalls, that derail far too many young people, definitely qualifies as over-communicating the MOST important messages.

Why is "No Communication" part of this chapter title? Silence can be deadly when it pertains to farting, but silence can be an extremely effective strategy when leading an organization. "Information overload" is a common flaw amongst college baseball coaches. Patience is your greatest attribute when coaching a new player. I inform our players in the first team meeting that coaches will observe and assess them for our first few fall practices, and maybe even longer, before we begin making fundamental technique adjustments. I took to heart Paul Molitor advising me over a Mai Tai in Maui, "not to change a player if they are good at something." I also have learned a larger body of viewed work is better than a snapshot when it comes to changing a player. Coaches are guilty of justifying their own existence by "coaching" non-stop like the aforementioned babbling chucklehead. Many coaches legitimately desire to help their players, but are unknowingly counterproductive because they offer too much information at one time. I firmly believe players learn quicker when tasked with one adjustment at a time. For example, a coach sees three changes necessary to improve a hitter, but attempts to correct all three flaws at once which actually impedes progress. The coach says to the hitter, "let's work on keeping your hands back longer, making your stride shorter, and opening up your stance." That hitter just became thoroughly confused and is now thinking through performance, which is a recipe for failure. Instead of this helpless coaching example, strive to fix the most egregious flaw that is most hindering a successful swing. Only move from one flaw to the next after the player has mastered your first adjustment. Sometimes the best coaching is no coaching. I'm certain Roy Hallenbeck had a lasting positive influence as Mike Trout's high school coach. Coach H has told me the best thing he did with Mike Trout's swing was NOTHING. I have previously mentioned some tremendous college hitters that I've had the privilege to coach. My greatest coaching feats with those special cats were writing their names in the lineup every game, and making sure they knew what time batting practice started!

"No Communication" plays a major role in my relationship with our pitching staff. I had the pleasure of working at a pitching clinic with Curt Schilling when he was the ace of the Philadelphia Phillies staff in the early 90s. Schilling had just completed a masterful 1993 post-season which included being named MVP of the National League Championship Series, and staving off World Series elimination for the Phils by twirling a 2-0 complete game shutout in game five vs. the Toronto Blue Jays. In the course of picking Schilling's brain about all things pitching, one comment he made stood out. He told me he was so locked in during games he didn't hear the crowd, and didn't want to be bothered by anybody. How does a guy not hear 60,000 screaming fans at a World Series game?!! Schilling went on to big game fame later in his career helping lead the Arizona Diamondbacks and Boston Red Sox to Worlds Series titles. I studied Schilling's clutch pitching performances from afar after our conversation, and I observed his competitive demeanor not only while he pitched, but also as he walked off the field after he completed an inning, and while he sat in the dugout between innings. "The zone" is a phrase reserved for athletes that are completely locked into competition, and are robotic masters of their craft while in "the zone." I was a young pitching coach when Curt Schilling taught me a lesson about being in "the zone," and I still apply that lesson today. I rarely talk to a pitcher during his outing unless an adjustment is needed, and definitely stay allergic to a pitcher that is in "the zone." This silent approach is communicated with the staff before the season begins so they don't feel slighted when they are ignored.

A recent example of the silent treatment happened during our 2019 conference tournament. Chris Wall, Columbia College's aforementioned ace, won our quarterfinal game with a dominating performance. He struck out 16 batters and came within one out of a no-hitter, before settling for a one-hit shutout in a 7-0 victory. Chris was in "the zone" and marched passed me after each of his eight no-hit innings while I stood at the end of the dugout. After the game, I had a friend in attendance that asked if I was superstitious, or didn't get along with Chris, since I never congratulated or fist-bumped him when he departed the field after each no-hit inning. I explained "the zone" to my friend, and also enlightened him that I make it a point to get along with guys that throw shutouts, while punching out 16, in playoff games! Another strategic silent treatment relative to the pitching staff is not communicating with them until the day after an outing, regardless if they authored a clunker, was an average Joe, or spun a masterpiece. Pitchers are emotional shortly after an outing, their short-term memory is cluttered, and they are less attentive. Pitchers know they won't hear from me immediately after their outing, other than the obligatory "great outing." The day after their outing, when the pitcher has had time to calm his mechanism, the coach/player communication is more civil, more honest, and certainly more productive.

Every leader embodies their own style, and every style is equally capable of being an effective communicator. Coaches are labeled stern disciplinarians, players' coaches, rah-rah motivators, quiet leaders, and numerous other descriptions. The constant variable for all leadership types is mastering the art of communication and no communication; while eliminating miscommunication and over-communication. Leaders should never be pretentious by creating a disingenuous persona, but should maintain their natural style while always striving to improve the important skill of communication. Remember to avoid babbling chuckleheads, refrain from calling the umpire a cocksucker, and last but not least, choose your words carefully if you are ever a game show contestant!

# Chapter Eight:
# The Chutzpah to be Contrarian

Contrarians are open-minded, curious, and creative visionaries that have the guts to take the road less traveled. Contrarians are just as likely to be called crazy as they are to be deemed brilliant. I personally find the Contrarian Philosophy to be sheer genius, as you will discover reading this chapter. Yogi Berra was one of Baseball's greatest players, but is equally famous for his head-shaking quotes. He turned one of those quotes into the title of his book, *"When You Come to a Fork in the Road, TAKE IT!"* Unlike Yogi's humorous and confusing play on words, I have taken the Contrarian road in Baseball and in life. "Conventional wisdom" is an overused phrase whose words have been strangely married for years. Conventional is defined as, "based in accordance with what is generally done." Wisdom is defined as, "the quality of having experience, knowledge, and good judgment." Why would a critical quality such as wisdom be applied to an act that is generally done? I view conventional wisdom as a conservative approach that lacks courage, but it limits one from being questioned or confronted. Second-guessing is every fan's inherent rite. Second guessers have never attended one of our practice sessions, doesn't know when a player is less than 100% healthy, and have zero knowledge of long-term motives related to player development; yet, they will second guess personnel and game strategy despite being completely ignorant. I would never walk into an accounting firm, executive board room, or construction site and second guess the decisions being rendered. Second guessers are prevalent in athletics, especially baseball, because a fan that has played little league baseball or watched a game on television is a self-proclaimed expert. Any organization or coach with a well-thought Contrarian plan will flourish once they don't give a damn about outsider opinion.

Las Vegas is the greatest blueprint for Contrarian success. The founding fathers for Sin City were ridiculed at the notion of constructing casinos in the middle of a Nevada desert. Their "crazy idea" has since been flipped into a gambling oasis that is one of the most-visited cities in the world that annually generates over a BILLION dollars of net income. For years Vegas has implemented well-thought strategies to sustain their financial juggernaut including complimentary alcoholic beverages to gamblers, using chips instead of currency to psychologically lessen losses, and creating a party ambiance that keeps customers coming back for more; despite habitually donating to the house. Slot machines have worse odds of winning than any other casino game, with the house holding a 3%-20% advantage. They are called one-armed bandits for a reason! A casino executive educated me on the value of slot machines during a Super Bowl party I attended in Vegas. While taking a leak, I was shoulder-to-shoulder with my next-door neighbors at the urinal and in real danger of another man's pee splatter. When I returned to our table I told our party host that they should have more room between the urinals. He nonchalantly replied, "More urinals means less slots. Urinals don't make us money."

Vegas' Contrarian genius also applies to sports betting which has long been one of the most popular vices for gamblers, and extremely profitable for casinos. The sports books' obvious built-in advantage is claiming 10% of all losing bets (known as the "juice" or "vig" in betting circles). Their hidden advantage is preying on the public's propensity to bet the favorites. Point spreads are analytically constructed by oddsmakers ensuring every contest is a 50/50 proposition, yet the public overwhelmingly still bets the favorites. Vegas refers to professional gamblers as sharps and the public as squares. The sharps realize betting the underdogs is often a financially prudent decision while the public continues its' relentless love affair with the favorites. One of my go-to books is *The Zen of Gambling* by Wayne Allyn Root, which emphasizes fearlessly betting the underdog. Mr. Root, dubbed the King of Vegas, is a professional gambler who was honored with a star on the Las Vegas Walk of Stars, which is a four-mile stretch on Las Vegas Boulevard honoring those people that have helped make Vegas famous. *The Zen of Gambling* is based on being Contrarian and having the chutzpah (extreme self-confidence) to pursue and execute your vision. Vegas' masterful Contrarian plan ALWAYS slants the odds heavily in favor of the house. The gambler's desperate plan is fumbling their last chip onto a roulette table while taking one final drunken stumble through the casino. Sorry if you have resembled the drunken stumble!

Many sports teams, like Vegas, have thrived thanks to taking a Contrarian approach. This approach is especially necessitated when teams have fewer resources, which usually results in less talent. A coach operating under such circumstances has two choices: Follow the masses and get their ass kicked, or adopt a Contrarian approach and enhance their team's probability for success. Two opponents that players and coaches dread are really talented teams, and teams that make them uncomfortable. Drastically altering normal game tempo has been an equalizer in basketball and football. Players become accustomed to playing at a universally adopted flow in their particular sport. Paul Westhead coached basketball at Loyola Marymount University and his teams played at an exhausting frenzied pace that gave opponents fits. Coach Westhead's Contrarian style led ESPN to create a 30 for 30 on Westhead entitled *Guru of Go*. Dave Arseneault, who coaches basketball at tiny Grinnell College, an NCAA Division 3 school in Iowa, implemented the Grinnell System which is a run-and-gun attack that implements a continuous full-court press, a bombardment of quick three point attempts, and substituting five new players every 30-45 seconds. Grinnell has won multiple conference titles and is the only NCAA Division 3 team ever featured on ESPN for a regular season game. Princeton University, under the guidance of Hall of Fame coach Pete Carril, was the polar opposite in regards to tempo. Coach Carril coached at Princeton for 30 seasons and popularized the phrase "Princeton Offense." Princeton's methodical half-court offense was built on backdoor cuts and lulling their opponent to sleep. In the 1989 NCAA Tournament, Princeton narrowly lost 50-49 to Georgetown, which was ranked number one in the country. Coach Carril's final collegiate victory was in the 1996 NCAA Tournament over defending national champion UCLA by a score of 43-41. Princeton competed with college basketball's bluebloods because Coach Carril had the chutzpah to be Contrarian!

Football is the ultimate game of bigger/faster/stronger wins. Leveling the playing field in football if you are not bigger/faster/stronger is as much about style as tempo. In today's college football a pass-happy spread offense is commonplace. However, Ken Niumatalolo still successfully employs the wishbone at the Naval Academy. The wishbone is an outdated run-heavy offense predicated on the quarterback making proper reads, and based on repetitive discipline from every offensive player. What better place to implement an offense based on DISCIPLINE than the U.S. Naval Academy! Coach Niumatalolo is popularly referred to as Coach Ken because his surname is challenging to pronounce. Navy's opponents find preparing for their wishbone attack just as challenging as Coach Ken's last name. The wishbone causes defensive coordinators sleepless nights and leaves defenders dizzy on game day. Chip Kelly created a name for himself at the University of Oregon from 2009-2012 by incorporating an offense that was the antithesis of Coach Ken's wishbone. Oregon's offensive goal was to take very little time between offensive plays, wear down their opponents by not giving them time for substitutions, and score as quickly as possible. Coach Kelly's offense-on-speed result-ed in a 2011 National Championship game appearance which they lost on a last-second field goal. Navy and Oregon can contribute their success to Contrarian coaches that definitely made their opponents feel uncomfortable.

Successful organizations have been built on Contrar-ian philosophy. The award-winning book-turned-movie,

*Moneyball,* is Baseball's greatest illustration of a Contrarian philosophy designed to compete with fewer resources. Billy Beane was the architect of "Moneyball" when he took over as the cash-strapped Oakland Athletics General Manager in 1998. Beane demanded his administration rely on new-wave metrics when evaluating players, and devalue the traditional five-tool scouting reports. *Moneyball* author, Michael Lewis, summed it up best, "I wrote this book because I fell in love with a story. The story concerned a small group of undervalued professional baseball players and executives, many of whom had been rejected as unfit for the big leagues, who had turned themselves into one of the most successful franchises in Major League Baseball." The Athletics were perennial contenders during the Billy Beane Era between 1998 and 2016 despite spending less than 100 MILLION DOLLARS in player salary than some of their chief competitors. I read *Moneyball,* and watch the movie, at least once a year because it's entertaining, but also because it's the ultimate in Contrarian motivation.

As mentioned earlier, recruiting has been the lifeblood for me rebuilding/building four college baseball programs during my career. Baseball has always been an arms race from Major League Baseball all the way down to Little League Baseball. The team with the best, and deepest, pitching usually wins. I have never met a coach that complains about too much pitching. Coaching staffs at all levels of baseball have probably begun commiseration after losing a hard-fought tournament with these seven words, "if we only had one more pitcher..." Any coach that has lost game one of a tournament, and attempted the long journey through the loser's bracket, can especially appreciate the baseball arms race. There is a reason starting pitchers are listed next to each team when you view a Major League schedule. It is because, quite simply, they have the greatest influence on the outcome of the game. Many sports books allow bettors to "specify" the starting pitcher for the team they are betting to win. Most college baseball programs sink the vast majority of their scholarship budget into pitching. After all, Baseball is an arms race...unless you are Coach Munns! My Contrarian organizational/recruiting epiphany came during my tenure at William Woods. Boomer and I were licking our wounds after losing yet another impact arm to a Division 1 school late in the recruiting process. At that time I made the bold decision to sink our scholarship money into good hitters rather than chronically repeating the frustration of playing the bridesmaid in the arms race. I had to be honest with myself and concede that quality arms resist NAIA Baseball to the very end. The past ten seasons, CONTRARY to popular belief, we have allotted roughly 75% of our scholarship budget to hitters, and an unheard of 25% to pitching. Why in the hell would anybody budget a 75/25 hitter/pitcher split if Baseball is an arms race?

Recruiting is an inexact science, and projecting amateur pitchers is one of the most difficult skills even for experienced recruiters. Pitchers also present a separate quandary; they are clearly Baseball's most important position, but are substantially more susceptible to injury than any other position. This two-pronged risk/reward equation makes evaluating and offering pitchers a delicate proposition. Hitters, on the other hand, are closer to a finished product when being evaluated, and don't have near the injury rate as a pitcher. Therefore, my epiphany meant paying for hitters to maximize our offensive production, while using fewer funds to secure the necessary pitching to win. Fortunately, my greatest strength as a coach is developing pitchers, and managing a pitching staff. Anytime you consider or construct a Contrarian plan you must self-analyze and ask questions relative to the plan. I asked myself, "what do hitters dislike other than an extremely talented arm with plus stuff?" I arrived at these three classifications that hitters dislike:

* Left-handed pitchers, especially soft leftys (those that lack pitch velocity)

* Pitchers with low arm slots, especially submarine slots

* Pitchers that throw their breaking ball for a strike

Why are leftys with ordinary stuff effective, and rightys with the same ordinary stuff glorified batting practice pitchers? This is Baseball's contribution to the greatest mysteries of the universe! Unfamiliarity for hitters plays a role in this baffling phenomenon. Roughly ten percent of the world is left-handed, and in the decade from 2011-2020 only 28% of MLB pitchers were left-handed. The percentage of leftys in college baseball is probably similar to MLB or even less. Bill Belichick, six-time Super Bowl-winning coach of the New England Patriots, annually sought advantage by employing a left-footed punter because it created reverse spin on the football, which made the punt less familiar and more difficult to receive for the opposing punt returner. The soft lefty has been torturing hitters for years. Hitter symptoms after experiencing "soft leftyitis" include breaking helmets, displacing water coolers, and profane tirades. A "comfortable collar" is baseball lingo for a hitter that has 0 (the zero resembles a collar) hits in his three or four at bats, but is very comfortable doing so because the opposing pitcher doesn't exhibit electric stuff. The "comfortable collar" often is strapped on a hitter by a soft lefty. Hall of Famer Tom Glavine earned 305 MLB wins, two Cy Young awards, the 1995 World Series MVP, and was a ten-time All Star. Not bad for a soft lefty! Jamie Moyer is perhaps the premier example of a soft lefty. Moyer tantalized hitters during his 25-year MLB career while winning 269 games. His ability to pitch with inferior velocity allowed him to perform at an advanced age despite not breaking a pane of glass with his fastball. Moyer earned his final victory at 49 years young, making him the oldest pitcher in MLB history to win a game. These two soft leftys never struck the fear of God in hitters, but were winners because they had gigantic cahonas and could hit a gnat in the ass from second base. "Crafty Lefty" is a term of endearment in the game of Baseball, and "Crafty Righty" is a term rarely uttered. A southpaw on the mound always gives you a chance to win!

The next hitter riddle from my "Big Three," is a pitcher that operates from a low arm slot. A conventional arm slot is over-the-top or three quarters. Hitters are comfortable (there is that word again) with these traditional arm slots, and have trained their eyes to focus on release points from these slots. A lower arm slot can transform a below-average pitcher into a relative out-getter, or better yet, into an all-conference performer. Any right-handed pitcher with pedestrian velocity and below-average stuff, is a candidate for a low arm slot in our program. "Headed to the basement" is a phrase adopted by Boomer, and refers to a right-handed pitcher that unknowingly will have his arm slot lowered sooner than later. Pitchers initially resist making this arm slot adjustment, but quickly endorse their new endeavor, when given the choice of pitching meaningful innings from a low slot or pitching zero innings from their preferred slot. The extreme basement dwellers are referred to as submariners, knuckle draggers, under-armers, and numerous other descriptions that more aptly identify a bowler than a pitcher. Hitters mutter under their breath, while shaking their head, anytime one of these pitching abnormalities is summoned from the bullpen.

The angle created by right-handed pitchers vs. right-handed hitters (right-on-right in baseball lingo) has the appearance of the baseball traveling sideways on a difficult angle from pitcher release point to the hitting zone. In essence, the right-handed hitter is tracking the baseball from behind him instead of identifying the pitch while it travels on a comfortable straight-line path from the traditional arm slot. The same is true for a left-on-left pitcher/hitter confrontation. Google John Kruk's comical at bat in the 1993 All Star Game vs. Randy Johnson for the ultimate example of low slot advantage. Kruk was one of the game's best hitters and he was rendered useless by the Big Unit's sidearm 100 mph fastball being released from a 6 foot 10 inch frame. This classic left-on-left battle of the mullets was entertaining for everybody except the Krukker, who likely shit his baseball pajamas! The pitcher that adeptly masters multiple slots becomes a slot machine nightmare for hitters. The degree of difficulty is already increased for a hitter when he faces an unfamiliar low slot, but that degree of difficulty is amplified vs. a pitcher that varies his arm slot from pitch to pitch. The slot machine is able to morph himself into two or three pitchers, and create continuous confusion during a hitter's at bat. Visualize a clock and imagine a right-handed pitcher's arm slot bouncing unpredictably between 1:00 and 5:00 every pitch, or a left-handed pitcher's arm slot doing the same between 11:00 and 7:00. Slot machines in Vegas stack the odds in favor of the house, and slot machines on the mound stack the odds in favor of getting outs.

The final cog in our trifecta is the power of the breaking ball. Curve balls, sliders, and cutters all fall under the breaking ball umbrella. I have met very few hitters that prefer hitting a breaking ball instead of a fastball. Quite simply, hitting a straight fastball is more desirable than hitting a pitch that curves, slides, or cuts. Special breaking balls earn titles like Uncle Charlie, Yellow Hammer, Yacker, Bastard Slider, Knee Buckler, and Pants Shitter among others. All hitters struggle vs. the special breaking ball, but many hitters still struggle vs. the average breaking ball. There are hitters who couldn't hit a breaking ball if they knew it was coming, but drool when fed a 100 mile per hour fastball. You can't sneak the sun past the rooster, and you can't sneak a fastball past good hitters! A sane person would never hunt a bear with a pocket knife, yet pitchers will persist on throwing more fastballs than breaking balls even when their fastball velocity wouldn't earn them a speeding ticket on a major highway. Pitchers inherently feel firing shitty fastballs at a hitter is more macho than attacking with a breaking ball. I argue that requesting a new baseball from the home plate umpire after allowing home runs, and backing up third base after allowing doubles, does not qualify as macho. A pitcher challenging hitters with below-average velocity is like a magician operating with a broken wand and dead rabbit. **Simple concept: Throw an abundance of breaking balls because hitters don't like hitting breaking balls.** When a pitcher is asked about his pitch repertoire his answer ALWAYS begins with "fastball." This common question/answer is recited universally as pitchers, catchers, and coaches become acquainted:

Coach or catcher asks, "What do you throw?"

Pitcher replies, "Fast, curve, slider, change."

The successful soft arm should list "fast" last. I have had countless velocity-challenged pitchers excel because they swallowed their pride and fell in love with the breaking ball philosophy. Coach Ken's wishbone makes defenses uncomfortable, Coach Carril's Princeton Offense makes college basketball teams uncomfortable, and breaking balls definitely make hitters uncomfortable. The best part about recruiting soft leftys, low slot arms, and breaking ballers...other schools don't remotely consider paying for their services. The trifecta is not sexy on the surface, but is a strong ingredient in our winning formula!

Hitting is all about timing and pitching is all about disrupting timing. The Tampa Bay Rays, and their manager Kevin Cash, introduced the "opener" in 2018. The "opener" strategy is also referred to as "bullpenning," and employs a starting pitcher who is typically a reliever, with the intention of that pitcher only recording a few outs before passing the baton to other members of the bullpen. The primary objective for this unique approach is never allowing a hitter to see the same pitcher twice. Cash's Contrarian pitching plan has been a contributing factor for the Rays being highly competitive despite ranking 28th out of 30 MLB teams in 2020 player payroll at $28,290,689. The New York Yankees, who lost to the Rays in the 2020 American League Championship Series, ranked first with a player payroll of $111,939,081. The Los Angeles Dodgers, who defeated the Rays in a tightly contested 2020 World Series, ranked a close second at $108,417,397. Quite an accomplishment to level the playing field with the big boys while staring at an 80 million dollar player payroll discrepancy!

"Johnny Wholestaff" is a term that has been used in college baseball for years to describe a team's plight when they lack a capable starting pitcher, but have a game scheduled. Game + no starting pitcher = Johnny Wholestaff. Mr. Wholestaff is comprised of staff bottom feeders, sore-armed starting pitchers on short rest, and ambitious position players willing to sacrifice their pitching virginity. Bullpenning is a completely different animal than Johnny Wholestaff. While both utilize a revolving door of relievers, bullpenning is a premeditated scheme to obtain 27 outs, and Johnny Wholestaff is concocting a dire list of suspects to serve up an inevitable beatdown. Bullpenning has been a personal way of life long before the Rays made it a polarizing baseball topic. My two key terms for successful bullpenning are "flip" and "contrast." My goal for a pitcher is to flip the opposing lineup (nine hitters) one time, and then insert a new pitcher that provides contrast. For example, start a soft lefty for the first flip, then insert a velocity righty for the second flip, followed by a soft submarine righty for the third flip, next up a funky lefty for the fourth flip, and last call is using our closer for the final outs of the game. Each hitter in the opposing lineup experiences an unfamiliar and contrasting arm for every one of his at bats. The 2015 William Woods Owls finished the season 39-14 and statistically had the second-best pitching staff in the country. We had exactly ZERO complete games thanks to a bullpenning approach led by our three-headed monster: James Ball (slot machine), Dylan Hastings (plus slider), and Ryan Yuengel (plus sinker). The three-headed monster featured stark contrast, and was a combined 18-4 with 12 saves and a 1.57 ERA. Cheers to Baseball, James Ball, Dylan Hastings, and Ryan Yuengel!

Taking the Contrarian bullpenning strategy to a new level is making pitching changes during the middle of a hitter's at bat, especially when the hitter has two strikes. The more pitches a hitter sees during an at bat, the more the advantage slants toward the hitter. I have enjoyed success employing this uber-Contrarian tactic vs. dangerous hitters. The mid-count pitching change draws quizzical looks from opponents and umpires, creates a murmur throughout the crowd, but usually results in an out. Bullpen utilization is the reason Major League Baseball will probably never see another .400 hitter. Ted Williams was the last hitter to achieve this difficult feat, posting a .406 batting average in 1941. The man nicknamed Teddy Ballgame was one the best pure hitters to ever step into a batter's box. He was one of the best fighter pilots to ever fly a plane. He was one of the best fly fishermen to ever cast a line. One human being is arguably the best in the world at THREE different skills? That's incredible! All due respect to the great Ted Williams, late in games he routinely faced a tired starting pitcher instead of fresh contrasting bullpen arms, which is why MLB has seen its' last .400 hitter.

Abner Doubleday is credited for inventing America's Past Time in a Cooperstown, New York cow pasture in 1839. I don't arbitrarily impose my Contrarian ways on Mr. Doubleday's grand game, but if I had the opportunity I would ask him one question that I've always pondered: Why did you decide the bases should be run counterclockwise? Can you imagine how drastically different baseball would be if first base and third base were transposed? Baseball supposedly has an invisible "book." A common expression muttered by coaches that lack a creative mind or guts is "that's what the book says to do" Coach Munns defiantly says, "F the book!" The baseball "book" has numerous silly rules that are blindly followed regardless of data, human variables; or God forbid, coaching instincts. Here are a few proverbs from the mythical 'book' followed by sensible reasoning to debunk the "book." NEVER attempt to steal third base with two outs...even though it is much easier to score from third base than second base with two outs. NEVER intentionally walk a player that is the tying or winning run late in a game...even though the player you are intentionally walking is a much better hitter than the player on deck. Corner infielders ALWAYS guard the foul line late in a game when you hold a one-run lead...even though you have overwhelming data that the hitter is highly unlikely to hit a ball down the line. My final Contrarian baseball lesson pertains to lineup construction. A lineup is as much a positive vibe as it is strategic. While I purposely plot on-base machines in front of clutch hitters, stagger our lineup with right-handed and left-handed hitters, and attempt to construct other built-in advantages; illogically shaking up the batting order on a bar napkin at Midnight can jump start an offense just as quickly. Billy Martin, long-time MLB manager that most notably served as skipper of the New York Yankees, was known to literally pull his lineup from a cap if the offense was slumping. Albert Einstein was one of America's most significant geniuses and he defined insanity as, "doing the same thing over and over and expecting different results." Mr. Einstein's prophetic quote applies to baseball lineups. Leaders should always lean Contrarian to reverse bad results.

Baseball legends have strayed from common fundamentals to achieve greatness by being Contrarian. Dan Quisenberry perfected the submarine delivery. Willie Mays patented the basket catch. Stan "The Man" Musial's batting stance looked like he was peeking around a corner. Chew on one of the greatest statistics in baseball history: Stan the Man had 3,630 career hits, 1,815 hits at home, and 1,815 hits on the road. Perhaps the greatest Contrarian success story in baseball is Pat Venditte's rise from walk-on pitcher at Creighton University to Major League pitcher. Venditte is the only switch pitcher in the history of Major League Baseball, proficiently able to pitch with both arms which earned him the nickname "The Octopus." He uses an engineered glove that fits each hand, and his ambidextrous prowess created the "Pat Venditte Rule," which requires any switch pitcher to declare which hand he will use before the at-bat begins. Venditte's standalone switch pitching was instrumental in his rise from college walk-on to The Show. I strongly encourage any aspiring leaders to ask themselves these questions while keeping a Contrarian open mind:

* Have I spent sufficient time in self-analysis?

* How will I build my organization?

* Where will I sink my resources?

* Who will I appoint as valued leaders in my organization?

Contrarianism made Quiz, Willie, and The Man great. Contrarianism catapulted The Octopus to The Show. Do you have the chutzpah to channel your inner Contrarian?

# Chapter Nine:
## They're Men Not Machines

Coaches that value building relationships with players maximize their team's ceiling for success. Athletes are live human beings whose actions are motivated by their emotions and feelings. They are not fictitious characters in a video game manipulated by a joystick or buttons on a panel. Hall of Fame MLB skipper Tony LaRussa was known for his permanent scowl, surly post-game press conferences, skin-tight baseball pajama bottoms, and staunchly defending his players at all times. TLR often mumbled a simple four-word answer when the media questioned a player's performance: **"THEY'RE MEN NOT MACHINES."** This chapter is dedicated to leaders psychologically connecting with their people, and why those four words should always take precedent. Obviously, the word "men" can be replaced with "women" or "people" depending on your team/organization. One strategy I religiously employ is talking to every player every day we have a team function (practice, game, study hall, off-season workout, etc.). An open-ended question that is simple, and **personal**, initiates coach/player interaction that goes a long way.

"How did you do on your test today?"

"How's your brother's high school football season going?"

"Are you deer hunting this weekend?"

"Are the Chiefs going to win Sunday?"

"How's your Grandpa doing?"

"Players' coach" is a phrase commonly used that carries a loose definition, and is interpreted differently by each user. The casual fan's first thought when they hear "player's coach" is the players like the coach. Good coaches prioritize being **respected** ahead of being **liked** by their players. I define "players coach" as, "a coach that genuinely cares about their players and grants them the autonomy to influence team initiatives." Unwavering and reciprocated trust between coaches and players is an essential mode of operation for successful teams.

"Honesty is the best policy" has been spoken by parents to their children for years, and is usually sound advice. However, there are a few exceptions to this age-old life philosophy necessitated by one's occupation. Undercover federal agents role-play "bad guys" to capture the world's most-wanted criminals. Professional poker players make their living by demonstrating an inconsistent pattern of play while bluffing their opponents. Greg Maddux was Baseball's ultimate poker player while deceiving hitters during his decorated 23-year MLB career. Maddux possessed below-average velocity, but combined pinpoint accuracy with superior pitch movement to become the only pitcher in Major League history with more than 3,000 strikeouts (3,371) and less than 1,000 walks (999). His ability to make the balls look like strikes, and make the strikes look like balls, baffled hitters and landed him in the Hall of Fame. The greatest mouthpiece for unfiltered honesty comes in the form of drunks and small children. I have witnessed this firsthand during a brief bartending career, and as a father of a six-year-old. A drunk at closing time will admire boobs out loud, remind fat people they are fat, and reveal their life story to complete strangers. Thanks to COVID-19, my daughter attended virtual kindergarten via Zoom, and I became the kindergarten teacher's aide. Not exactly what I had in mind for the Fall of 2020! During one of our first class sessions, I informed Mary Ellen I was going to the restroom and would return shortly. The restroom is within earshot of our home classroom, and I heard Mary Ellen proclaim to the class, "My Daddy is on the dumper, and our cat Ozzie is trying to push the bathroom door open." While a drunk's honesty is impolite, and Mary Ellen Munns' honesty is definitely too much information; I prescribe to a more tactful version of "honesty is the best policy" when dealing with players.

I verbalize an open door policy, and encourage players to walk in my office anytime they feel the need to discuss anything. Playing time, or PT as it's universally abbreviated, is the most common reason a player pays a visit to my office. Jon Fogerty's 1985 hit song, *Centerfield,* features the famous lyric that sums up the feelings for any player that has ever sat the bench, "Put me in coach, I'm ready to play today." Fans sing along as *Centerfield* blares over loud speakers at ballparks of all levels, including every Atlanta Braves home game before Braves players take the field in the first inning. *Centerfield* is popular because the message personally resonates with listeners who at some point in their life, at some level, on some team, in some sport, have served as a glorified spectator wearing a uniform. I use the following five-point checklist that is instrumental in granting a player's request to "put me in coach"; work ethic, positive attitude, class attendance/effort, off-field behavior, and performance. I'm a firm believer in equal opportunity practices, which make playing time decisions an easier proposition. Every player on our roster receives an equal amount of repetitions rather they are an All-American or they have played sparingly. Pitchers all throw equal number of bullpens. Hitters all take equal rounds of batting practice. Infielders all take equal amounts of ground balls. Outfielders all take equal amounts of fly balls. Catchers all catch an equal amount of bullpen sessions. There are college baseball programs, especially at the Division 1 level, where some pitchers don't throw bullpens in the presence of the pitching coach, and some hitters don't take batting practice on the field. This asinine practice plan not only eliminates fair competition for playing time, but as importantly, stunts the development of players (usually young players).

Players often begin the playing time conversation by asking, "How do I get more playing time?" My reply is always, "You don't **get** playing time. You **earn** playing time." Coaches in other sports can lean more on objective data when determining playing time. Wrestling coaches have a wrestle-off in every weight class before an upcoming match. Track and cross country coaches make decisions dictated by times on their stopwatch. Golf coaches rely on the lowest scorecards from practice rounds. While many would consider writing a baseball lineup a subjective task, it's actually closer to an objective task thanks to my five-point checklist and conducting equal opportunity practices. I tell our players that they determine who plays, I merely write their names on a lineup card. Words have never rung more true than the adage, "the hardest people to judge are yourself and your children." Players disregard the facts when assessing their position on the depth chart, and will even question why they are sitting behind a teammate that is clearly more deserving. These are examples of common replies I've given that use the five-point checklist as a reference: "If you were in my shoes, would you play a guy hitting .400 or a guy hitting .180?" "If you were in my shoes, and two players were close in ability level, would you play a guy that has never missed a team function or a guy that hasn't been as committed to the program?" My friends that are supervisors in Corporate America, and higher education, dread administering annual employee performance reviews more than they dread the eve of a colonoscopy appointment. I truly believe they would rather drink laxative Kool-Aid and shit their brains out than spend precious time preparing vanilla documentation to cover their employer's ass. This cookie cutter formality is predominantly disingenuous, informs employees what they **want** to hear and always recommends an area for improvement even when unnecessary. Jesus himself would struggle to receive a perfect grade on an annual employee performance review! Honesty is definitely the best policy in the coach/player PT conversation, and players are informed what they **need** to hear.

Preferential star treatment happens frequently in Major League Baseball because all player contracts are **guaranteed**, which usually **guarantees** players will exert less effort. Star players put butts in the seats which generate millions of dollars for ownership; thus they are granted preferential treatment. Not to mention the manager is making substantially less money than the star players. Name another occupation where the supervisor's salary pales in comparison to those they are supervising? Unlike professional sports, college coaches hold all the leverage with their players. Scholarships are **not guaranteed,** and can be revoked for habitual insubordination. Coaches also influence their star player's professional future by providing them ample playing time, and recommending them to professional organizations. Tim Corbin (Vanderbilt Baseball), John Calipari (Kentucky Basketball), and Nick Saban (Alabama Football) currently are coaches at powerhouse college programs, in their respective sports, that serve as middlemen for aspiring millionaires. These superior leaders have built the necessary pedigree to demand effort from their star players. As a result, their star players will "run through a wall" for their program.

Hall of Fame coach Jimmy Johnson built the Dallas Cowboys dynasty of the early 90s that won three Super Bowls in four seasons (1993, 1994, and 1996). Johnson famously cut backup linebacker John Roper for falling asleep in a meeting. His quote when he was later asked about cutting Roper epitomizes preferential star treatment, "I can't be writing what the rules are because my rules vary from player to player....In Dallas we had a linebacker named John Roper who got cut for falling asleep in a meeting. If Troy Aikman (the Cowboys Hall of Fame quarterback) fell asleep in a meeting, I'd go over and whisper, 'Wake up, Troy'" I was coaching at Drexel when Jimmy terminated Mr. Roper's employment with the Cowboys. Coach Maines was a stickler for being on time and was known to leave any Drexel player behind that was late for the team bus, regardless of their status. Players knew when the clock struck departure time the wheels on the bus were rolling. Coach Maines was part-amused, part-disgusted, but fully understanding of Jimmy Johnson's actions. We had a running joke after the Jimmy Johnson/John Roper incident that mocked preferential star treatment. Coach Maines would look across the bus aisle at me and whisper, "Is Frenchy on the bus?" I would nod my head, and then he would order the bus to depart. Our odds of winning significantly increased if Drexel's version of Babe Ruth, who was capable of throwing a shutout and going four for four, was on board for the trip. In all seriousness, if the real Babe Ruth was late for the bus he would have been left behind because Coach Maines knew preferential star treatment at the college level is a recipe for long-term team dissension. Fair and consistent treatment of players affords coaches a platform to positively impact the players they coach, long after the players are done playing.

Our greatest gift as leaders is the impact we have on others. What coach, teacher, or mentor had the greatest impact on you? I was unknowingly shaped as a person, and prepared for my future profession, by my high school basketball coach, Mark Scanlon. Coach Scanlon taught me life lessons in Mexico High School's cramped, dingy, bandbox of a gym that resembles fictitious Hickory High School from the classic hoops movie, *Hoosiers*. After much thought, I have chosen to elaborate on four attributes that Coach Scanlon instilled in me that are required for any meaningful endeavor. The foundation for his program was WORK ETHIC. We were in better physical condition than our opponents thanks to the grueling pre-season sprint workouts prescribed by Coach Scanlon. His version of boot camp stretched diaphragms to unchartered limits, reintroduced the fetal position, and transformed trash cans into puke receptacles. We practiced unceremonious drills including diving for loose balls, taking charges, and sprinting back on defense. DISCIPLINE was demanded, without exception, during the pre-season, practice sessions, and games. **Every** player touched **every** line during wind sprints or **everybody** repeated the entire set of wind sprints. A gag order was in place while players practiced free throws. Eliminating conversation ensured game-like focus while practicing an essential, yet monotonous, skill that determines the outcome of close basketball games. I mandate a gag order when our players practice bunting for the same reason. A player that received a technical foul in a game received an automatic ticket to the bench for at least a quarter. Coach Scanlon is one of the most COMPETITVE human beings I've ever encountered. He despised losing! His practices the day after a loss were grounds for cruel and unusual punishment, and the gymnasium at Mexico High School was not a desired destination. The final attribute I learned from Coach Scanlon was FUN. How can descriptions like boot camp, puke receptacles, and gag order be associated with the word fun? Answer: When the preparation (practice) is instrumental in amplifying the game day experience and achieving great results. Simply put, winning is more FUN than losing! The following clichés apply to preparation in Athletics:

* If you fail to prepare, prepare to fail.

* Practice is for the coaches and games are for the players.

* The practices are work and the games are the reward.

My practical experience learning work ethic, discipline, competitiveness, and fun as a high school basketball player was the first step in my ongoing education to become a better college baseball coach. One sport uses a ball that resembles an inflated pumpkin, and the other sport uses a hand-held pearly white sphere wound together by 108 red stitches. Two completely different sports using two completely different balls, yet both are capable of assisting one another in teaching valuable life lessons. Single-sport specialization is when a child or adolescent focuses on only one sport, and trains year-round exclusively for that particular sport. I completely disagree with this narrow-minded thought process. Parents and youth coaches are doing youngsters a disfavor by attempting to predict their athletic future while chasing a college scholarship. A premeditated choice of sport lends itself to burnout, and the child may be forced to disregard their eventual favorite sport, or their eventual best sport. Rickey Henderson, Joe Mauer, and LeBron James were all incredible high school football players. Henderson is widely considered the greatest leadoff hitter in MLB history and is the game's all-time stolen base leader. Mauer is the only high school athlete to be selected *USA Today* Player of the Year in two sports (baseball and football). He is also the only catcher in MLB history to win three batting titles. King James is shattering NBA record books and is debated as the greatest basketball player of all time. Can you imagine if these sports legends foolishly "single-sport specialized" in football? I am forever grateful for Coach Scanlon's tutelage and cherish my high school basketball memories. Cheers to Baseball and Coach Scanlon!

Coaches with properly prioritized motives have a moment in their career when they realize that positively impacting other people is more important than their win/loss record. My moment thankfully came early in my career, and was provided by former Drexel player Ryan Ross. Ryan and I were reminiscing good times at one of his teammate's wedding receptions when he told me, "Coach, I want to thank you for making a big difference in my life. You recruited me to play baseball, which is why I attended Drexel. I met my wife at Drexel. My degree from Drexel is why I have a good job." Ryan was a ball-hawking Gold Glove centerfielder who was instrumental in the success of Drexel Baseball, and his heartfelt thank you was instrumental in helping define my career mission. Cheers to Baseball and Ryan Ross! George Kissell spent 69 years in the St. Louis Cardinals organization as a scout, coach, manager, and instructor. Mr. Kissell was a baseball lifer credited for being the primary influence for creating the "Cardinal Way," which is an organizational manual designed to guide Cardinal players. I created the "Cougar Way," which are the eleven pillars that guide Cougar coaches and players.

## The Cougar Way

* Family **ALWAYS** comes first.

* Players and coaches have fun.

* Academics are a top priority. All players understand and commit to the Columbia College Baseball Academic Action Plan.

* Adopt a team community service initiative that makes a difference in people's lives.

* Have a positive attitude **EVERY** day. Excuses and negativity are the tools for losers.

* Be a great teammate. Do something every day to make a teammate better.

* Practice like you play in your biggest game (focus, energy, competitiveness).

* We have "no tolerance" lack of effort guidelines. We **ALWAYS** play harder than our opponent.

* Demand attention to detail with Columbia College Baseball game nuances (offense, defense, pitching, base running).

* Coach individualism in players within a fundamental program framework.

* Create a culture, instilling Cougar Pride, which transcends when a player becomes an alumni. Columbia College Baseball will **ALWAYS** be a special second family for alumni.

By design, the first pillar and the final pillar in "The Cougar Way" emphasizes "family." Players are excused from any team function, including the biggest games on our schedule, for all things family-related. Attending a younger sibling's high school championship game, serving as a groomsman, or paying respects at a funeral far outweigh any baseball game. **THEY'RE MEN NOT MACHINES!** A student-athlete's life is consumed by their academic experience, their athletic experience, and their social experience. The third experience listed is the one most overlooked by college coaches. I encourage the social experience by not scheduling team functions on the weekends during our off-season (October-December). Down time for our players stoke their passion for the game and counteracts burnout. The social experience is critical for building team camaraderie; which players, in retrospect, will ultimately value the most. Pay attention the next time you hear a retired professional athlete asked what they miss most about the game. The answer is usually, "the camaraderie with my teammates," "hanging out with the guys," "the brotherhood in the locker room," or similar words communicating the same message. Leaders who are cognizant of the social experience facilitate team camaraderie, which translates to better results.

Former players' wedding receptions celebrate that day's matrimony, and double as baseball reunions. Bro-hugs, smiles, and laughter dominate these priceless gatherings. The funny stories told are like a classic comedy movie you have seen numerous times; they never get old, and top laugh levels are reached (refer to Chapter Six, page 120, if you need to reacquaint yourself with the Munns seven-tier laugh ladder). Former William Woods player, Damon Adrian's, wedding reception was a snapshot of what college baseball is all about. A proper introduction for professional wrestlers includes their hometown, weight, and recognition if they are a champion or former champion. Those grapplers wearing a mask, or appearing deranged, have long had their hometown designated "whereabouts unknown" as part of their shtick. Damon is from Mary's Home, MO, where there are more cattle than people, two-lane black-top roads are considered major highways, and "whereabouts unknown" is an appropriate description for those trying to locate it on a map. Damon shared apartment AA-6 with five teammates during his time at William Woods. Here is the roll call for Damon's roommates, with hometowns listed in parentheses: Bobby Butvin (Mantua, OH), Kyle Muzechka (Vegreville, Alberta Canada), Nick Spagnola (Chicago, IL), Kyle Switzer (Columbus, GA), and Kale Wierenga (Lacombe, Alberta Canada). Quite a diverse six-pack of characters that had convened in Mary's Home! Excluding Damon, the five other lads had never heard of William Woods University before being recruited, and sure as hell never visited Mary's Home. They all arrived on William Woods' campus to continue their dream of playing college baseball and departed as members of a lifelong brotherhood. Three of the AA-6 posse commemorated their special bond by being branded with an "AA-6" tattoo! Cheers to Baseball and the AA-6 Boys!

John Thompson was one of the most successful college basketball coaches of all time, but the positive impact he had on his players is what makes him a role model for all leaders. He was a 6'10" menacing mountain of a man whose eyes cast a competitive glare down on his players, opposing players, opposing coaches, and officials. Big John roamed the sideline with his trademark white towel draped over his shoulder while he coached the Hoyas. His teams replicated his personality and competitive spirit. The Hoyas were physical and played defense like their lives depended on it. Coach Thompson **changed** Georgetown University from a 3-win afterthought into a national powerhouse during his 27-year tenure as their Head Coach (1972-1998), highlighted by winning the 1984 national championship. More importantly, he **changed** the lives of his players. Allen Iverson starred at Georgetown before becoming an NBA superstar for the Philadelphia 76ers. During Iverson's Hall of Fame induction speech he sobbed, "I want to thank Coach Thompson for saving my life." Big John refined AI's pull up jumper and killer crossover dribble, but improving one's basketball skills are inconsequential compared to saving one's life. An isolated act during the 1982 national championship game is part of college hoops history and defines Coach Thompson. Georgetown's Fred Brown inexplicably passed the ball directly to North Carolina's James Worthy, with the Hoyas trailing by one point, and less than ten seconds left in the game. Brown's turnover cost Georgetown a shot at winning the national title, and is considered one of sports' worst blunders. Big John, conscious of the big picture, consoled Brown during his lowest moment with an elongated hug immediately after the game. **THEY'RE MEN NOT MACHINES!** John Thompson passed away on August 30, 2020. His death elicited an overwhelming outpouring of love and thanks from former Hoyas/basketball icons including Iverson, Patrick Ewing, and Alonzo Mourning. College basketball coaches nationwide draped a white towel over their shoulder for the opening game of the 2020 season in honor of Coach Thompson. The towel tribute for Big John epitomizes the saying, "imitation is the greatest form of flattery."

The fear of failure is worse than failure itself. When a player overcomes the fear of failure, and learns to cope with failure, they greatly enhance their odds for future success. Michael Jordan recited this lesson during a 1997 Nike commercial, "I've missed more than 9,000 shots in my career. I've lost almost 300 games. Twenty-six times I've been trusted to take the game-winning shot, and missed. I've failed over and over and over again in my life. And that is why I succeed." Hitting a baseball is the ultimate exercise in futility. The best hitters in the world post a .300 batting average. It bears repeating, how many other activities are applauded for achieving a 30% success rate? Striking out has sadly become more acceptable in today's game of baseball, but the act of making an out without putting the ball in play is still the most demoralizing out for a hitter. How they recover from strike three dictates their fate for future at-bats. Reggie Jackson is MLB's all-time leader in strikeouts with 2,597 whiffs. He is also a member of Baseball's prestigious 500 Home Run Club, smashing 563 dingers to place 12th on the all-time list. Reggie is a prime example of failure being the reason he succeeded. Stay tuned....plenty more to come about Reggie.

"Never" is a tenuous word, and "never say never" is sage advice with few exceptions. You should NEVER ask a lady if she is pregnant. You should NEVER catch without a cup. I have a Never Theory that applies to baseball players. I remind our players constantly they are NEVER as good as their good, and they are NEVER as bad as their bad. What the hell does my twisted repetitive Never Theory mean? One performance does not define a player. The message is to stay humble after your very best performances because they are unfortunately not sustainable, and stay confident after your very worst performances because they are thankfully not sustainable. Rick Wise is the unofficial spokesperson for my Never Theory. Wise pitched nineteen seasons in the big leagues for five different organizations. For my money, he recorded the greatest single-game performance in MLB history on June 23, 1971, as a member of the Philadelphia Phillies vs. the Cincinnati Reds, when he became the only player to throw a no-hitter and hit two home runs in the same game. Wise was also the winning pitcher for the Boston Red Sox in Game Six of the 1975 World Series, which many baseball historians consider the greatest World Series game ever played. Two incredible days in the career of Rick Wise! Even more incredible considering his career record as a pitcher was 188-181. How does a pitcher that is slightly above average accomplish two of the greatest feats in MLB history? Because players are NEVER as good as their good!

Collecting 3,000 career hits is a testament to a Major League hitter's ability and durability. The 3K Hit Club is rarified air, with only 32 players in the history of the game earning membership. The 3K Hit Club is also a near-automatic ticket to baseball immortality. 30 of the 32 players that have amassed at least 3,000 hits have a bronze bust of their likeness residing in Baseball's Holy Grail, which is the National Baseball Hall of Fame and Museum in Cooperstown, NY. The only two players excluded are Pete Rose (Baseball's all-time hit king with 4,256 hits), who is ineligible because of his lifetime ban for gambling on baseball; and Rafael Palmeiro (3,020 hits) who was blackballed after steroid allegations. Bill Buckner collected 2,715 hits during his 22-year MLB career, while playing for five different organizations. However, Billy Buck is most known for his 10th inning error in Game Six of the 1986 World Series while playing first base for the Boston Red Sox. His infamous miscue allowed the winning run to score, and the Red Sox would subsequently lose Game Seven to the New York Mets, which extended their title drought to sixty-eight seasons. How does a borderline Hall of Famer allow a groundball to roll through his wickets with a World Series at stake? Because players are NEVER as bad as their bad.....except for Ron Wright.

Wright played eleven seasons of professional baseball, and appeared in ONE Major League game as the Seattle Mariners Designated Hitter on April 14, 2002. Wright was hitless in three plate appearances, and "achieved" the dubious trifecta of striking out, hitting into a double play, and hitting into a triple play. Why the Baseball Gods elected Ron Wright to be their poor bastard by serving him a triple-decker shitburger is beyond me; but nonetheless, he is the lone exception to my Never Theory because he NEVER got an opportunity to redeem himself. Please don't interpret my description of Ron Wright as criticism. I commend him for persevering eleven seasons in the minors before debuting as a big leaguer. I also salute him for playing in ONE Major League game because it's one more Major League appearance than Darren Munns and 99% of the population that has ever attempted to play baseball. As cruel irony would have it, Mr. Wright's dreadful one-game career happened on Pete Rose's birthday. Charlie Hustle won the hit race vs. Ron Wright 4,256 to 0. **THEY'RE MEN NOT MACHINES!**

Which comes first, success or confidence? A person

needs success to gain confidence, yet confidence breeds success. Are you confused yet by this dizzying question? Take a break from reading, dive into deep thought, and attempt to decipher which came first in your occupation, hobbies, past sports you played, or any other meaningful endeavor. This is the thought-provoking sister question to "Which came first, the chicken or the egg?" Success and confidence positively enable each other when developing baseball players. I utilize both to initiate the process, so I guess my answer is "all of the above!" Here are examples of how success comes first, and how confidence comes first:

*Success before Confidence:* Coaches can choreograph their practice plan to create success for players, which develops their confidence. During our fall season and pre-season, I will schedule a pitcher that lacks confidence to face our three or four worst hitters, and I will schedule a hitter that lacks confidence to face our worst pitcher. These premeditated mismatches, unbeknownst to our players, provide immediate positive feedback, and the caliber of their practice opponent/teammate is irrelevant. I gradually graduate the player to more challenging practice opponents as the player experiences success.

*Confidence before Success:* Our players are my greatest resource for supplying a confidence boost. During daily hitting drills, I will pair a talented hitter that lacks confidence with an established veteran hitter who is a team leader. I will schedule a talented pitcher that lacks confidence to throw his bullpen session to an established veteran catcher who is a team leader. Before that day's practice, I speak with the established player and inform them to "coach up" the player that lacks confidence. I will even issue this stern pre-practice ultimatum with our established player, "I don't care if he is good or bad, make him feel like he is the best player in the country by the end of practice." Players, and especially young players, are motivated by their established teammates more than their coaches. Leaders coaching their people....to coach their people....is the best form of delegation.

A player's confidence level can be improved, but players are either born with clutch DNA or born without clutch DNA. The five senses are an amazing gift bestowed upon most humans. Hearing, sight, smell, taste, and touch are powerful mechanisms that steer our daily existence. I am perplexed by the following three conundrums provided by the human senses that apply to many people, including Yours Truly:

* We have to turn down the volume on our car radio to look for a house number when searching for an unfamiliar residence.

* The copycat reflex applies when we see another person yawn or vomit. Thankfully, I only fall victim to yawning.

* We gag, use the collar of our shirt as a fart-guard, and overact when another person has gas; yet are not offended whatsoever by our own foul gas.

I am also perplexed by the powerful sixth sense in Athletics which is being clutch. Peyton Manning authored the most fourth quarter comebacks of any quarterback in the history of the NFL (43 comebacks). When asked about pressure he replied, "Pressure is something you feel when you don't know what the hell you're doing." Easy for Peyton to say! The majority of athletes wage psychological warfare between their ears, and their butthole puckers at the mere thought of performing in the clutch. Only a select few have a pulse that beats in slow motion, and ice water running through their veins, when the game is on the line. Possessing the "It Factor" is a unique and special quality!

The ability to thrive under pressure has built players' reputations and defined their legacies. Hall of Fame quarterback, Joe Montana, led the San Francisco 49ers to four Super Bowl victories and was renowned as a clutch performer. In Super Bowl XXIII the 49ers trailed the Cincinnati Bengals 16-13, and took over possession of the football on their own eight-yard-line with 3:20 left in the game. While in the huddle before the drive started, Montana pointed out comedian John Candy in the crowd to his teammates. How many players are in relaxation mode, and panning the crowd with the Super Bowl hanging in the balance? Joe Cool proceeded to march the 49ers on a game-winning 92-yard drive to win the Super Bowl. Robert Horry played sixteen seasons in the NBA for four different organizations. Horry won seven NBA championships, the most by any player in the modern era. Despite posting a modest career scoring average of 7.0 points per game, he earned the nickname "Big Shot Rob" because of his knack for clutch shooting in the post-season.

The New York Yankees and Boston Red Sox form one of the most heated rivalries in sports, let alone baseball. From 2003 until 2014 Derek Jeter and David Ortiz shared center stage, for the Yankees and Red Sox respectively, in this longstanding rivalry. The Captain and Big Papi's baseball resumes speak for themselves, but it's their propensity for performing in the clutch that separates them from other great players. Hitters that possess the "It Factor" seem like they come up every time the game is on the line, and they are polarizing figures for fan bases. Derek Jeter is revered by Yankees fans, but was serenaded with "Jeter sucks" every time he visited Fenway Park. Big Papi is a baseball god in Boston, but always received a resounding Bronx cheer at Yankee Stadium. These rabid fan bases detested Jeter and Ortiz because The Captain and Big Papi repeatedly tortured their rivals with clutch heroics. The home team in baseball traditionally wears white uniforms, and the road team wears colored uniforms. Pete Rose relished being booed by opposing fans and viewed it as respect. Charlie Hustle once said, "I always say, the only time you gotta worry about getting booed is when you're wearing a white uniform. And I've never been booed wearing a white uniform."

My personal favorite clutch performer is the aforementioned Reggie Jackson. Baseball's World Series is played in October, and Reggie earned the nickname "Mr. October" for his post-season exploits in the Fall Classic. Raucous home crowds chanted "Reg-gie, Reg-gie, Reg-gie...." in unison every time he stepped into the batter's box. Reggie's majestic home runs AND his strikeouts were must-see TV! He cemented his post-season legend, and nickname, during Game Six of the 1977 World Series by launching three home runs...on three pitches...vs. three different pitchers. Reggie is the only player in World Series history to accomplish this incredible three-pitch / three-home run feat, and his World Series heroics led the Yankees to a title vs. the Los Angeles Dodgers. Mr. October dripped with brash bravado, bordering on cocky, as he strutted his way to five World Series championships. Reggie was twice named World Series MVP, had arguably the most complimentary nickname in the history of Major League Baseball, and even had a candy bar named after him. Reginald Martinez Jackson embodied the "It Factor!" Am I a fan of Reggie? My only child was going to be named Reggie if she would have entered the world as a boy. Instead, my daughter was tagged with the family name Mary Ellen. I told Mary Ellen, "I might start calling you 'Reggie' because that was going to be your name if you were a boy." She replied, "Daddy, I like the name Mary Ellen a lot better." Even though my six-year-old daughter doesn't prefer the name Reggie, I prefer players that have Reggie-esque clutch tendencies.

Coaches can't transform their players into Joe Cool, Big Shot Rob, The Captain, Big Papi, or Mr. October; but they can identify those players that have clutch DNA, and those players plagued by Butthole Pucker Syndrome (BPS). Analytics is more prevalent in Baseball than at any time in its' history. All aspects of America's Pastime are leaning on technology for measuring players. Pitches register a spin rate. Batted balls register a launch angle. Unfortunately, cutting-edge Baseball analytics has not created a pucker rate that measures how a player responds to clutch situations. Can you imagine if scouts and coaches asked the question, "What's his pucker rate?" I pay close attention to each of our players' "It Factor" as I learn our team. A player that has BPS can still be an asset, but a coach must reduce pressurized situations for that player during competition. All pitchers are not wired to record the last three outs of a baseball game. For example, I remove starting pitchers, who suffer from BPS, sooner than later to eliminate them attempting to get big outs late in a game. They still help the cause, but aren't stretched into an area of the game they can't handle. Many college and professional relievers are proficient at pitching the eighth inning, but struggle to knock down the ninth inning. When a team designates an 'eighth inning guy' that often means he doesn't possess the onions to pitch the ninth inning. A player's batting average with **R**unners **I**n **S**coring **P**osition is my favorite offensive individual player metric. RISP is a telltale acronym to evaluate clutch hitting. A talented hitter that struggles with RISP can help the team, but don't expect him to flourish hitting in the middle of the lineup. I bury that hitter in the bottom of our lineup where expectations are lessened, and pinch hit for him in late-game pressure situations. The player with chronic and severe BPS is virtually useless as tits on a bull, and destined to appear in blowouts only.

The "feel factor" resides in all of us. How do you genuinely feel while watching a player perform in the clutch? Heading into the 2021 NFL season, Patrick Mahomes owns a 44-10 record as the Kansas City Chiefs starting quarterback, and in four of his ten losses, the opponent scored on the last play of the game. He is 6-2 in three post-seasons, including winning the Chiefs first Super Bowl in fifty years. He became the first quarterback to erase double-digit deficits in three consecutive post-season wins during the Chiefs Super Bowl run. His only post-season losses were vs. the New England Patriots in the 2018 AFC Championship Game, who scored on the last play of the game in overtime, and vs. the Tampa Bay Buccaneers in the 2020 Super Bowl. Mahomes is only three seasons into his NFL career, and already has played in three AFC Championship Games and two Super Bowls. How do football fans genuinely feel when Patrick Mahomes is taking snaps with the game on the line? Professional golf tournaments are played in four days, consist of seventy-two holes (eighteen holes per day), and are usually played Thursday through Sunday. Tiger Woods is the greatest closer in the history of golf. Tiger owns a 45-2 career record when holding an outright lead through fifty-four holes, and is 56-4 when at least sharing the lead. The four golfers that prowled with Tiger on day four and emerged victoriously are in select company, and can brag to their grandkids! How do golf fans genuinely feel when Tiger Woods holds a lead on Sunday?

Former Columbia College player, Ethan Howser, definitely possessed the "It Factor." I genuinely felt confident when Howie stood in the batter's box and determined our fate in big games. Howie was in the first recruiting class for Columbia College when I started the program. He had played one season of junior college baseball before quitting the game he loved. The descriptions "head case" and "bad attitude" were attached to Howie's name when I did my homework during the recruiting process. Thankfully, Howie is from the same hometown as my college roommate/teammate DeWayne Hickey. Howie's Dad and DeWayne were very good friends. I called Hick and received a ringing endorsement from a trusted voice. Hick told me, "Ethan's a great kid and a helluva player. Just hates losing, has a temper, and needs some structure. He would be fine in your program. You need to get him." It's a small world, and an even smaller world in college athletics! Cheers to Baseball and DeWayne Hickey! Howie was completely misunderstood by his critics. The transition from high school to college is challenging for all teenagers, but was especially challenging for Howie. During his junior college career he lost his Dad to cancer and had major elbow surgery. **THEY'RE MEN NOT MACHINES!**

Hick's recommendation and prediction were on the money. Howie learned to cope with failure, became a team leader, was a three-time all-conference player, and had a flair for the dramatic as a Columbia College Cougar. He was our leadoff hitter for the first home game in the history of our program. You only get one chance to make a first impression, and Howie welcomed Baseball to Columbia College by hitting the first pitch he saw for a home run. Talk about a grand entrance! Howie's junior season we trailed conference rival Lyon College 5-3 with one out, and two men on, in the bottom of the seventh inning of a seven-inning game. Howie blasted a three-run walk-off homer vs. the eventual Conference Pitcher of the Year to secure a 6-5 triumph. Howie saved his best for last his senior season. Prior to the first game of our post-season conference tournament, I asked Howie the rhetorical question, "Howie, we ready to roll today?" As he used a Sharpie pen to write "DAD" on his taped wrists, he looked me square in the eye and nonchalantly replied, "I got this Coach." He then promptly did his best Mr. October impersonation by going five for five and belting three home runs, leading us to a 9-5 win. Howie kick started a post-season run that propelled us to the first-ever National Tournament in program history. Cheers to Baseball and Ethan Howser!

A roster full of clutch players preserves a coach's job security, and a roster full of players suffering from BPS will get a coach fired. However, both deserve to be equally respected as people, and both can feel the same lifelong positive impact from a leader that has their priorities in order. Ethan Howser's future wedding reception/baseball reunion excites me more than any clutch home run he ever hit! As a coach, employer, friend, or parent always keep in mind **THEY'RE PEOPLE NOT MACHINES!** The world's most sinful heathens can recite the Golden Rule that resides in Matthew 7:12 from the Holy Bible: "Do unto others as you would have them do unto you." Reverend Munns suggests an even better Golden Rule: "Do unto others **even better than** you would have them do unto you." I don't think tweaking the Golden Rule is blasphemous, but at the risk of getting struck by lightning, please quickly turn the page to Chapter Ten.

# Chapter Ten:
## Knowledge Is Key

The Intelligence Quotient, better known as IQ, is a metric designed to assess human intelligence. I would venture that if you polled 100 random people, less than 50% even know what the I and Q represent in this two-letter acronym. IQ tests assign a number to test-takers which signify that person's intelligence. IQ tests reveal that approximately two-thirds of the population scores between 85 and 115, approximately 2.5% score above 130, and approximately 2.5% score below 70. There are plenty of layman shithouse psychologists that forego the scientific intelligence quotient, and use popular phrases to assess intelligence. "The smartest guy in the room" is high praise. "I'm not a rocket scientist, but..." is a frequent self-deprecating comment when beginning a sentence. A few derogatory sayings include, "dumber than a box of rocks," "the elevator doesn't go all the way to the top," "not the sharpest knife in the drawer," and my personal favorite, which once got me in hot water, "shit for brains." My wife mandated that I join her, on a Saturday afternoon, for a one-day eight-hour childbirth class as we neared the arrival of Mary Ellen Munns. During one segment late in the class, we were learning the art of properly applying a diaper on an infant mannequin. I was mentally drained, had checked out hours ago, and thought it would be humorous to strap a diaper on the mannequin's head. The nurse/teacher did not find it amusing and sternly informed me, "Sir, this is a very important parenting skill and I would appreciate that you take it seriously." I replied, "If the child is anything like her father, I expect a real "shit for brains," and she will need to wear the diaper on her head." The class erupted in laughter, my wife shook her head, and Nurse Hardass was appalled.

What I do take seriously is my passionate, ongoing, and never-ending pursuit of baseball knowledge. Remember me mentioning that leadership seminar I attended years ago and the keynote speaker stated, "You bring three things with you every day: your people, your **knowledge**, and your attitude." The speaker's statement opened my eyes to the three leadership "controllables.: A person's knowledge level, unlike general intelligence measured by an IQ test, can be applicable to specific skills, occupations, or any activity requiring thought process. I readily acknowledge my baseball IQ measures significantly higher than my general IQ. Alex Trebeck hosted the ultimate knowledge-based game show, *Jeopardy,* for thirty-seven years before his death on November 8, 2020. The legendary quizmaster relegated me to dumbass status anytime I attempted to play as a viewer, but I would take my chances to become a *Jeopardy* champion if the categories were all baseball-related. RIP Mr. Trebeck! Surgeons will score higher on an IQ test than the vast majority of college baseball coaches. However, most surgeons lack the **baseball knowledge** necessary to successfully function as a college baseball coach. Side note: Keep in mind that a future surgeon finishes last in every medical school's graduating class. Pray to God the last-place graduate is not wielding the scalpel for your surgery! A popular Holiday Inn Express commercial depicted a bumbling surgeon standing over his patient upon completion of surgery. The surgeon pulled his mask down, and one of the nurses observed, "You're not Dr. Stewart." The imposter assuredly announced, "No, but I did stay at a Holiday Inn Express last night," and departed the operating room. While the commercial is creative and shines a positive light on a hotel chain; there is no substitute for knowledge...even if you stayed at a Holiday Inn Express last night!

Branch Rickey was a player, manager, executive, and owner during a 50-year career in Major League Baseball. Mr. Rickey astutely observed, "Baseball is like church, many attend but very few understand." His observation is not limited to spectators, but also applies to players and coaches. Why should we hang on Branch Rickey's every word? Mr. Rickey was a respected baseball pioneer who designed the model for Baseball's minor league farm systems and introduced the protective batting helmet. He is most famous, and rightfully so, for breaking MLB's color barrier when in 1947 he signed Baseball's first black player, Jackie Robinson. Branch Rickey practiced "Black Lives Matter" generations before it became a slogan for social justice in 2020. Mr. Rickey's signing of Jackie Robinson was larger than Baseball. It was a signature moment in sports history, and in the history of the United States. Baseball historians habitually debate if today's players are better than players in the "Babe Ruth era?" I steadfastly argue that today's game, and collective player pool, is far superior because Jackie Robinson broke the color barrier. MLB's All Star Game, known as the Mid-Summer Classic, is a collaboration of the game's biggest superstars. The 2019 All Star Game's starting rosters (eighteen hitters and two starting pitchers) featured eleven players of color and nine Caucasians. All due respect to The Babe, yesteryear's players pale in comparison, IN MORE WAYS THAN ONE, when compared to today's current players. "Baseball IQ" is an overused, and subjective, description of a coach or player that is considered an advanced student of the game. A baseball coaches' lifelong quest for knowledge is vital to improving their Baseball IQ, and enables them to join Branch Rickey's select group of those that understand.

I attribute three sources that originally generated my Baseball passion, and initiated my Baseball learning curve: Whitey Herzog, Jack Buck, and Strat-O-Matic Baseball. As a kid growing up in mid-Missouri I was a diehard St. Louis Cardinals fan. At the impressionable age of twelve, I was blessed that the Redbirds hired Whitey Herzog as their manager in 1980. Little did I know, for the next decade the White Rat provided Cardinal Nation a daily tutorial on how to manage a baseball game. Whitey was playing chess and opposing managers were playing Chutes and Ladders! I had the pleasure to meet Whitey on several occasions, one being when we both spoke at the Missouri State High School Coaches Convention. Needless to say, Munns was on the undercard and the White Rat was the main event! I asked Whitey to sign a baseball for my Dad, and he immediately obliged. As he penned a personalized autograph that became one of my Dad's most-prized possessions, he said, "This ain't nothing. I had to sign twenty dozen golf balls last weekend. You ever try and sign your name on a golf ball?" Whitey's wit, charisma, and Baseball IQ made him one-of-a-kind. I revere Whitey Herzog, and am grateful for the influence he unknowingly had on a future college baseball coach growing up in small-town Mexico, MO. Cheers to Baseball and Whitey Herzog!

A baseball play-by-play broadcaster is the direct link between a Major League team and their fan base. The special squawkers are fountains of baseball information, master storytellers, and make listeners feel a personal connection with them. Jack Buck called Super Bowls, World Series, and numerous other major sporting events during his Hall of Fame career; but his distinct voice was synonymous with Cardinals Baseball. I was one of many that felt a personal connection with Jack Buck. He brought the game to life for his radio listeners. Jack Buck was with me when I tucked my tiny transistor radio under my pillow, and I dozed off to the Redbirds playing late games two time zones removed on the West Coast. Jack Buck was with me for family barbecues. Jack Buck was with me for long car rides. Jack Buck instructed Cardinal Nation to, "Go crazy folks, go crazy!" when Ozzie Smith hit a walk-off home run to defeat the Los Angeles Dodgers in Game Five of the 1985 National League Championship Series. Did Jack Buck have an influence on me? Chew on this fact: Other than my parents, I listened to Jack Buck more than any other person during my upbringing. Jack's crowning moment came when he delivered a moving speech, and read his poem titled, "For America," before a Cardinals game on September 17, 2001, just days after the United States suffered the 9/11 terrorist attacks. His speech and poem were remarkable, but more remarkable considering he was severely stricken with Parkinson's disease, so frail he could barely stand upright, and passed away less than a year later on June 18, 2002. Jack Buck celebrated every Cardinals victory with his signature line, "That's a winner!" Mr. Buck was the real winner! Jack passed the broadcasting torch to his award-winning son Joe Buck, and he passed his love for Baseball to Cardinal Nation. My knowledge and love for Baseball largely stems from my "relationship" with Jack Buck. Cheers to Baseball and John Francis "Jack" Buck!

Here are my three favorite baseball broadcasters not named Jack Buck that were also baseball educators for their fan bases:

* Vin Scully called Dodgers games for 67 seasons before retiring in 2016 at 88 years young. Mr. Scully is a wordsmith extraordinaire, operated without a partner, and his smooth narrative style felt more like a bedtime story than a baseball broadcast. Mortal announcers fill their broadcast with dead air. Dead air did not exist during a Dodgers broadcast. Vin Scully informed listeners interesting back-story details about players; such as another sport they played in high school, college accomplishments, hobbies, etc. I would listen to Vin Scully read the greater Los Angeles phone directory just to hear his voice!

* Harry Caray spent over fifty years broadcasting baseball for five different organizations, but it was his final sixteen seasons spent with the Chicago Cubs (1982-1997) that earns him inclusion on my list. Harry was the ringleader of a wild party 81 times a summer with 40,000 of his "closest friends" at Wrigley Field. Every home game he would serve as

the conductor and lead the crowd in a slobbering rendition of "Take Me Out to the Ballgame" during the 7th inning stretch; while half-cocked, full of Budweiser, and sporting his trademark oversized spectacles. Harry sprinkled "Holy Cow" into each broadcast whenever he found something **amazing**. "Holy Cow" was liable to be bellowed while he marveled at a sensational play, wished Gladys from Peoria a happy 100th birthday, or admired a pair of voluptuous double Ds hanging out in the bleachers. His personality made the hapless Cubbies fun to watch, and that **amazing** feat alone deserves a "Holy Cow" salute!

* Ken "The Hawk" Harrelson has manned the Chicago White Sox booth for the past 33 seasons. The Hawk refers to the White Sox as the "good guys," and he is regarded as the greatest homer in the history of broadcasting. There are countless "Hawkisms," illustrating his bias for the White Sox. The Hawk roars his patented, "You can put it on the board! Yeeeees!" when a White Sox player homers. Happy Hawk is known to celebrate stellar Sox plays with "Hell yes!" or "Mercy!" Dejected Hawk reacts with "Dadgummit!" or "You gotta be bleeping me!" when he feels the White Sox got shafted by an umpire's call. The Hawk relates to fans drinking a beer at home because he sounds just like them while broadcasting a Sox game. He tells listeners right before the first pitch of every broadcast to "sit back, relax, and strap it down." I suggest you "sit back, relax, and strap it down" for *MLB Network's* one-hour documentary, "Hawk: The Colorful Life of Ken Harrelson." You will understand why Ken "The

Hawk" Harrelson is beloved by fans on the South Side of Chicago, and is a Baseball treasure.

Strat-O-Matic Baseball is a board game that was invented in 1961 by Bucknell University student, Hal Fichman, and is a precursor to today's video games. Strat-O-Matic uses statistical data to replicate player performance, and makes the gamer feel like they are managing a Major League contest. I logged thousands of Strat-O-Matic games as a youth with Todd Spessard, my childhood buddy and fellow baseball addict. We were solely responsible for selecting our starting lineups, making pitching changes, and all other tactical strategies that occur during a baseball game. Cheers to Baseball and Todd Spessard! I even played Strat-O-Matic Baseball by myself! I managed both teams, kept player stats, and proclaimed "That's a winner!" when the last out was recorded in my fictitious game. Choosing the computer as your opponent was not an option for a child of the early 80s playing a board game! My love affair with Strat-O-Matic Baseball continued into my college years where I formed leagues with my teammates, and we dueled every waking moment for Strat-O-Matic bragging rights. *MLB: The Show* is today's updated version of Strat-O-Matic Baseball. I constantly overhear the players in our baseball program forecast, boast, and bitch about their performance playing the popular video game with their teammates. MLB informational player cards and dice were the provided props for playing Strat-O-Matic Baseball. They have been replaced by spot-on MLB player mannerisms, and detailed animation, brought to life by *MLB: The Show*. Although there is a generational gap between Strat-O-Matic Baseball and *MLB: The Show,* the common denominator between the games is what matters most: both share Baseball as the theme that facilitates team bonding amongst college teammates. My Baseball IQ received an educational boost at an early age thanks to Strat-O-Matic Baseball. Cheers to Baseball and Hal Fichman!

"Professional development" is a catchphrase used in all occupations whose purpose is to improve one's knowledge and skills. Ultimately, each professional determines their commitment to their personal development. The American Baseball Coaches Association (ABCA) is the national organization for baseball coaches of all levels. Over 5,000 baseball coaches flock to the annual four-day ABCA National Convention, whose location rotates major cities each year. The ABCA National Convention is the professional development Mecca for baseball coaches. I have attended numerous conventions, and quickly realized that coaches' motives vary during their four-day professional development excursion. I have observed six classifications of conventioneers whose personal agendas contrast greatly while searching for "professional development." I challenge coaches that have attended the ABCA National Convention, and those readers in other vocations, to visualize the following six-pack of characters. Do these folks exist at your professional development gatherings?

> \* Suckass: He is on a four-day ass-kissing mission in hopes of landing a better coaching job. It is highly recommended he packs extra lip balm!

> \* Party Animal: He has a scouting report for every bar, nightclub, and strip joint weeks before the convention kicks off. He watches the morning

session through bloodshot eyes, while battling a splitting headache, and stationed near a water cooler in the back of the convention ballroom...if he's even able to answer the bell from last night's shenanigans.

* Panhandler: The ABCA has an exhibit hall filled with booths of vendors hustling their baseball-related products and gimmicks. The Panhandler spends his entire convention filling out raffle tickets, and negotiating/begging with vendors to supplement his baseball program.

* Family Vacationer: He has one foot in the grave of his coaching career, and has graduated from Suckass, Party Animal, Panhandler, or all of the above. His First Lady joins him for an all-expenses-paid "professional development" experience/family vacation.

* True Professional: He is a rare bird that is strictly business, and actually attends for the **sole** purpose of becoming more professionally developed. He wears a permanent scowl, takes copious notes on the front row, and clutches his tattered briefcase like an undercover spy delivering top secret information. He is uber-dedicated, but will never be confused as the life of the party!

* Old Timer: I love this guy! He is retired and relishes the opportunity to talk baseball with anybody that will lend an ear. The convention is his pride and joy. He becomes aroused (no blue pill required) as each year's convention approaches on the calendar!

The scheduled clinicians selected by the ABCA are brilliant baseball minds from the high school, college, and professional ranks. They have dramatically nurtured my Baseball IQ over the years. However, I have learned as much from impromptu clinics conducted nightly in the hotel bar, which becomes a baseball think tank that is jam-packed with grown men vehemently discussing America's Past Time. Power points presented in the convention ballroom are substituted with tavern clinicians diagramming plays on high-top bar tables for their peers. Salt shakers, pepper shakers, and empty longneck bottles represent baseball players. A drink coaster marks home plate and sugar packets serve as three bases. Coaches jot useful tips on cocktail napkins to reference when they return home from the convention, and also to reference the next morning when too many empty longnecks cause them amnesia! Happy hour turns into closing time in the blink of an eye as baseball coaches attempt to answer all of Baseball's questions in one evening. Here are three examples of topics that will precipitate spirited debate lasting hours:

> Should your catcher call his own game or a coach call pitches for him?

> Should there be a Designated Hitter or should pitchers hit for themselves?

> Should Pete Rose be in the Hall of Fame?

For the record, I believe catchers should call their own game, I'm in favor of the DH, and HELL YES Charlie Hustle deserves induction into the Hall of Fame! The bartender declaring "last call" is the only stoppage for passionate baseball coaches talking shop. My Mother-In-Law claims, "nothing good happens after midnight," but I argue the impromptu bar room baseball clinics are an exception to her rule! As a reminder, Joaquin Andujar's favorite word was "**youneverknow.**" **You never know** from whom, or where, you will gain valuable knowledge.... and that includes a hotel bar room after midnight.

Kansas City Chiefs Head Coach, Andy Reid, is considered an offensive genius and one of the shrewdest play callers in the history of the National Football League. Coach Reid adheres to the previously mentioned concept of never knowing from whom, or where, you will gain valuable knowledge. He openly takes play suggestions from his top offensive players, and recently revealed that while he was an offensive assistant for the Green Bay Packers (1992-1998) he used a touchdown-producing play suggested by a janitor. I advise leaders to utilize all resources for maximum enhancement of their organization, and never underestimate the validity of an inexperienced voice. A young intern's voice may be the voice of a future CEO, and a young assistant baseball coach's voice may be the voice of a future respected baseball mind. I met native Philadelphian, Chris Calciano, when he joined Drexel's coaching staff as a volunteer assistant. Chris was a baseball junkie consumed 24/7 by the "why" for every aspect of the game. We thoroughly relished engaging in spirited debates regarding Baseball's finest fundamental details. Little did I know that my spirited debates were with the future Professional Scout for the Boston Red Sox. Chris is a great friend, valuable resource, and I am forever grateful that our paths crossed during the infant stages of our careers. Cheers to Baseball and Chris Calciano! If a janitor can dial up a touchdown for the Green Bay Packers then surely we should all keep our ears wide open in our continued quest for knowledge!

Here's a simple concept: Baseball coaches can expand their knowledge by **watching** baseball. I am flabbergasted by the number of baseball coaches that ignore watching their chosen craft. Viewer access through television packages, and social media, is more prevalent than ever before. *MLB Network* is a 24-hour daily network that serves as a round-the-clock instructional video for ambitious baseball coaches. Knowledgeable hosts, past MLB executives, and former MLB players dissect the game, and disseminate useful tidbits in an entertaining format. *MLB Network* is Baseball Utopia for fans, and a powerful 24/7 resource for coaches. One of the gravest mistakes baseball coaches make is specializing in only one aspect of the game. College coaches are often labeled "hitting guys" or "pitching guys," and these specialists can earn a handsome living in college baseball. However, head coaches, and leaders in general, significantly upgrade their leadership capabilities by becoming knowledgeable about all factions of their organization. The CEO of a company, or head coach of a college baseball program, needs to know the "why" for every program objective. I purchase Direct TV's Extra Inning package to access every Major League game played all season long. Pure bliss is hibernating in my basement, and devouring a smorgasbord of MLB games. I become the czar of the remote control, and rabidly bounce from game to game. Channel surfing MLB games is a joyous act of fandom, but my man cave also serves as a laboratory for professional development. I isolate on numerous baseball nuances while stalking the entire slate of MLB games. Studying the best players in the world on an 85-inch flat screen is virtual learning at its' finest! My ass also prefers the soft leather recliner in my home "classroom" as opposed to an uncomfortable desk chair provided in traditional classrooms. I pay attention to a plethora of "games within the game" while viewing Major League Baseball. I have prioritized a few "games within the game" from hitting, defense, and pitching that are critical variables for determining overall success.

## HITTING

Hitting a baseball is arguably the hardest act in all of sports, and requires multiple moving body parts working in unison from head to toe. Let's focus on three swing essentials when hitting a baseball. 1) What does a hitter use as his pre-pitch? Pre-pitch is the moment in time a hitter occupies before the pitcher gets to his release point. Pre-pitch rhythm is a preparatory routine that initiates the hitting process before a hitter actually swings their chosen weapon. Hitter pre-pitch mechanisms include gyrating hands, waving the bat slowly back and forth over home plate, and waggling the bat on the back shoulder. 2) How does a hitter stride? Strides for hitters range from no stride at all to an exaggerated high leg kick. Regardless of a hitter's stride preference, they cannot be late getting their front foot down, or hitting becomes impossible. "Get it down early" is frequent reinforcement from Boomer to our hitters, and is one of the staples for our hitting philosophy. Getting the front foot down early allows hitters to handle velocity, and eliminates lower half distraction while identifying pitch type and pitch location. 3) Where are a hitter's eyes during their swing? Vision is the most underrated and overlooked (no pun intended) attribute for an athlete, especially when attempting the ultimate hand-eye challenge of hitting a baseball. A common fundamental flaw in beginning hitters is seeing the pitcher through tilted, or slanted, eyes. A hitter's head should be turned, with both eyes looking directly at the pitcher, while in his hitting stance. This simple technique ensures hitters use optimal vision, as opposed to peripheral vision, during their swing. You wouldn't turn sideways when the optometrist asks you to read an eye chart, so why would you turn sideways when attempting to hit a baseball? A picture-perfect swing is accomplished when the hitter reaches the point of contact staring down the barrel of their bat, and they physically see their bat strike the baseball. Youth coaches verbalize plenty of cockeyed information to youngsters, but "keep your eye on the ball" is never bad advice.

I spared you a complete anatomical breakdown of swinging a baseball bat at the risk of you closing the book; and simplified the process by choosing pre-pitch, stride, and vision. I'm fully aware there is more to hitting a baseball than the three aforementioned aspects of the swing. Professional and college hitting coaches formulate complex hitting philosophies that incorporate detailed swing mechanics. However, the most established coaches would agree that pre-pitch, stride, and vision are common requirements to successfully hitting a baseball. Little leaguers, college hitters, big leaguers, and even Wiffle Ball players all become more "hitterish" upon mastering pre-pitch, stride, and vision. Mike Trout, Juan Soto, and Nolan Arenado are three of my favorite "subjects" to analyze during my professional development home sessions.

These hitting machines combine plate discipline and power while consistently producing at a high level. Streaky hitters can get hotter than two squirrels humping in a wool sock, but can't hit a beach ball off a tee while enduring a prolonged slump. Coaches know there is an expiration date for streaky hitters, but unlike a gallon of milk, the future expiration date is a mystery. Trout, Soto, and Arenado don't have expiration dates because they are hand-eye freaks of nature, and because they methodically repeat their pre-pitch routine, habitually get their front foot down early, and maintain vision throughout the entirety of their swing. They are the best hitters in the world and ONLY fail 70% of the time!

## DEFENSE

The opposing lineup's 39th man to bat in a nine-inning game is the most dangerous hitter of the game. Why the 39th hitter? Because the 39th man up in a baseball game is the 3-hole hitter batting for the fifth time, and that at-bat usually occurs in the ninth inning. The batter occupying the third spot in a lineup is traditionally a team's best hitter. During Baseball's early years, a player's uniform number represented where they hit in the lineup. Babe Ruth wore number three, and Lou Gehrig wore number four, while hitting third and fourth for the New York Yankees. Hitter #39 is avoided by throwing strikes and playing solid defense throughout the course of a game. Every base on balls donated by the pitching staff, and every error committed by the defense, increases the odds of a date with Hitter #39. Therefore, recording two outs by throwing one pitch is especially beneficial in eliminating Hitter #39's appearance. The double play (DP) has long been nicknamed, "A Pitcher's Best Friend." The twin killing turns jams into scoreless innings and neutralizes the game's best hitters. The career GIDP (grounded into double play) leader board is a who's who list of MLB legendary players. Longevity, turtle speed, and loafing to first base all contribute to becoming a maestro of the GIDP. Albert Pujols sits atop the leader board with 399 career GIDPs and counting. I highly doubt Albert will halt play and request the baseball commemorating his 400th GIDP!

Most DP ground balls are a five-step process (catch-throw-catch-throw-catch) that entails three catches and two throws in the following chronological order: **catch** the ground ball, **throw** the baseball to second base, **catch** the baseball, **throw** the baseball to first base, and **catch** the baseball. One glitch in this simple five-step process and a pitcher is betrayed by his best friend. Second basemen are the recipient of the first throw more than any player during a GIDP involving three players. The most invaluable DP advice I received came during my first year of coaching from Coach Maines. He teaches second basemen to place their left foot in the middle of the rightfield side of second base, and take their **right foot to the baseball** while receiving the first throw of the DP. Most MLB second basemen turn DPs flat-footed, or use a soft pitter patter, because they possess superior arm strength to complete the DP. Amateur second basemen more likely require a short step with their right foot to gain momentum for their throw to the first baseman. GIDPs are a hot topic during my professional development man cave sessions. I attentively study, and usually rewind, every DP turned while watching an MLB game; focused on all DP details including footwork, underhand/overhand feeds, and middle infielders transferring the baseball from their glove to their throwing hand while completing the DP. One pitch producing two outs deserves my undivided attention!

A routine ground ball fielded by a professional or college infielder, with a man occupying first base, results in two outs. Therefore, keeping the double play in order is a top defensive priority. An obvious prerequisite for GIDP is having a runner on first base. Two factors that keep the double play in order are controlling the running game and outfielders hitting their cutoff man. Pitchers control the running game by varying how long they hold the baseball before delivery. A pitcher's unpredictable "hold pattern" makes it difficult for runners to time the pitcher when attempting to steal second base. Pitchers also must have a delivery quick enough to allow the catcher to throw out a would-be thief. A pitcher's time to the plate is measured with a stopwatch. The stopwatch is started on the pitcher's first movement, and ended when the timer hears the pitch hit the catcher's mitt. Veteran scouts and coaches calloused thumb pads take a beating timing pitcher's deliveries. An ideal time required to control the running is 1.0 - 1.3 seconds. A time above 1.3 seconds increases the chance of a stolen base, and increases the chance a pitcher doesn't get to see his best friend. "Hit your cutoff man" is screamed by frustrated coaches at outfielders. An outfielder missing his cutoff man has ruined double play opportunities, and caused grown men to throw child-like tantrums, since the inception of Baseball. Here is the game scenario that drives coaches bat shit crazy: runner on second base, routine single hit directly at an outfielder, outfielder overshoots his cutoff man while throwing home, batter/runner that should be on first base advances to second base, THE DOUBLE PLAY IS NO LONGER IN ORDER, and Hitter #39 is looming!

# PITCHING

The pitching rubber is seventeen inches long and can be utilized by hurlers to maximize control and pitch action. I learned a semantics lesson relative to the pitching rubber from a ten-year-old while working at the Princeton University Baseball Camp early in my career. As I stood atop the mound on the pitching rubber and prepared to demonstrate, I asked a group of beginning pitchers, "How many of you have used the rubber?" A ten-year-old camper snickered, "I haven't yet, but my older brother uses them with his girlfriend." The young fellow was thinking condoms and I was thinking pitching! To this date, I reference the seventeen-inch slab, which is the pitcher's starting point, as the "pitching rubber," and not the "rubber." Home plate is also conveniently seventeen inches wide, creating a sixty foot-six inch symmetrical invisible tunnel between the pitching rubber and home plate. A pitcher is allowed by rule to position themselves anyplace within the seventeen inches. Where a pitcher stands in relationship to the pitching rubber is something I always observe while watching baseball.

The simple act of establishing a starting point on the pitching rubber is a vital element in determining success.

For example, a right-handed pitcher who features a plus breaking ball is best served to start on the extreme third base side of the pitching rubber. This starting point makes his plus breaking ball even better because the baseball's flight path is directly at a right-handed hitter before breaking into the strike zone. A different right-handed pitcher, whose best pitch is a power sinker that moves toward a right-handed hitter, is better served to use the first base side of the pitching rubber as his starting point. This starting point allows his pitch movement to jam right-handed hitters, instead of plunking right-handed hitters if he were positioned on the third base side of the pitching rubber. Using the pitching rubber to maximize pitch action is similar in principle to arm angle advantage that was previously detailed in the book. I analyze pitch repertoire and pitch action during the introductory stage of coaching a pitcher, and then "suggest" where they should stand on the pitching rubber. The answer usually given by pitchers when asked why they stand on a particular part of the pitching rubber is, "I don't know." Assisting pitchers to choose an advantageous starting point is better than letting them arbitrarily choose a starting point. I have two final pieces of advice pertaining to the pitching rubber: 1) Experiment with pitchers' starting points on the pitching rubber. Determine which starting point they throw the most strikes, and determine which starting point maximizes their pitch action. 2) Always use the term "**PITCHING** rubber" instead of simply "rubber" when coaching young pitchers!

I cannot watch an MLB game without predicting every pitch type, and pitch location. Pitcher vs. Hitter is the essence of Baseball, and the ultimate game of cat and mouse. Smart fingers trump a cannon arm on the priority list for catchers in our program. Calling a game from the recliner is mentally engaging, and constantly challenges one's mind relative to pitch sequence, pitcher's strengths, and hitter's weaknesses. Our catcher's call their own game, but during the pre-season, we have bi-weekly meetings with our catching staff to discuss every pitcher on our roster. These sessions are an open dialogue for all catchers and coaches to learn the pitching staff. We rank each pitcher's pitch repertoire from best to worst. Ancient Baseball advice is, "Don't get beat with your worst pitch in a big spot." We want to make sure our catchers unanimously know pitch rank for every arm on the staff. We identify how to attack right-handed hitters and left-handed hitters, which are two entirely different activities. For example, a pitcher's breaking ball might be serviceable vs. a right-handed hitter, but forbidden vs. a left-handed hitter, or vice versa. We discuss the psyche of each pitcher, and the most appropriate ways to handle them during an outing. Finally, and most importantly, the conversation is brutally honest and confidential. The following comments are typical during our catcher meetings:

* "His slider is way better than his curveball. He needs to shit can the curve ball."

* "He likes an early target when he throws his fastball away to a righty."

* "You have to remind him to mix his hold pattern with a runner on first."

* "He's not ready to get big outs yet."

* "He responds to an ass chewing when he is struggling."

My Baseball knowledge has been stimulated by Whitey Herzog, Jack Buck, Strat-O-Matic Baseball, the ABCA convention, bar room clinicians, and watching the game. However, our **players** throughout the years have unquestionably taught me more about Baseball than any other resource. This is especially true while talking Baseball with the great hitters I've had the privilege to coach. I gain helpful knowledge from an offensive standpoint, and from a pitching perspective, when I ask great hitters open-ended questions: "How often do you guess pitch type or inside/outside location?" "How did you put such a good swing on that 3-2 slider?" "What is your least favorite pitch to hit?" The knowledge I gain is used to coach other team members. You have probably figured out by now that I have a tremendous affinity for Pete Rose. My favorite lesson from Charlie Hustle is his six ways for a hitter to gain advantage: choke up on the bat, choke down on the bat, crowd the plate, back off the plate, move up in the batter's box, and move back in the batter's box. All due respect to Baseball's Hit King, I learned more from listening to Andrew Warner during his two-year career at Columbia College than I learned studying Pete Rose for a lifetime. Andrew was also a catcher with valedictorian fingers which qualified him as a double-edged savant in the game of Pitcher vs. Hitter. Blind leaders in Baseball, and the "real world," fail to utilize their in-house resources. Your best player is obviously a tremendous asset, but a leader's ability to gain knowledge from their best player makes **everybody** on the team better.

The pursuit of knowledge about one's passion lasts a lifetime. Nobody dies with their think tank completely full. The leading experts in their chosen field are closer to a full tank than others when the casket closes, but their knowledge level still does not measure 100%. One of my favorite Baseball proverbs is, "Every time you attend a game you see something you've never seen before." I especially enjoy hearing these words uttered by a Baseball lifer, which is proof we are never done learning. I opened this chapter discussing IQ and sharing several laymen shithouse psychologists phrases to assess knowledge, or lack of knowledge. I'll close by repeating my favorite derogatory assessment, and sharing another popular saying that sums up the chapter: Don't be a **"shit for brains,"** and recognize that **"knowledge is the key to success."**

# Chapter Eleven:
# Old School Connecting with Generation Z

"Old school" describes proud traditionalists that revel in steadfastly not changing their ways. "Old school" is the elder statesman in a pickup basketball game wearing a headband, goggles, nut hugging shorts, bulky knee braces, high socks whose elastic is on life support, and canvas Chuck Taylor high tops. He is the last guy picked to play, but a likely candidate to calmly drain a game-winning set shot to decide the contest. "Old school" in the workplace is the employee who operates on clockwork routine. They arrive at the same time every day, park in the same spot every day, and pour their coffee in the same mug every day. They don't give a damn that their wardrobe is outdated and resembles an outfit worn at a throwback 1980s costume party. A yellow notepad substitutes for a laptop computer, yet despite their resistance to technological advancements, they remain one of the company's most reliable assets. *Old School* was even chosen as the title for the 2003 hit comedy starring Luke Wilson, Vince Vaughn, and Will Ferrell who, as men in their 30s, relive their college days by starting a fraternity. The trio recruits a motley crew of fraternity brothers from all walks of life. The senior member of their newly formed fraternity is 88-year-old Joseph "Blue" Pulaski played by Joseph Cranshaw. During one classic scene from *Old School,* Blue is standing in a blow-up baby pool filled with KY jelly, and prepared to tangle with two young attractive females in a wrestling match. Will Ferrell has the dual role of ring announcer and referee while overseeing this ridiculous stunt. Blue orders the "referee" to "Ring the bell you fuckin' pansy!" and then promptly topples over backwards to his death. Please let the honorary Joseph "Blue" Pulaski's final words serve as the official introduction for *Cheers to Baseball's* final chapter.

Today's generation of young people ranging in age from nine to twenty-six has been dubbed Generation Z. How do "old school" coaches bridge the gap with the Generation Z era? The first step is recognizing changes in today's **players** and today's **game**. "He can't relate to today's **players**," and "the **game** has passed him by" are frequent comments directed at "old school" college baseball coaches. We all know people in life that not only resist change, but fear change, even when change improves their situation. They refuse to switch occupations. They refuse to depart their hometown. They refuse to divorce themselves from a bad relationship. They refuse to **CHANGE**! I am flattered when 'old school' is attached to my name, and consider it a term of endearment, but I also realize my "old school" ways must be adapted to Generation Z. Leaders are understandably apprehensive about changing their proven process. I strike a delicate balance maintaining the core values of our process while evolving with the game, and most importantly, staying connected with Generation Z. Nearly three decades of my life have been devoted to concocting a blueprint for operating a successful college baseball program, yet my livelihood is equally reliant on my ability to annually connect with a new group of 18 to 23-year-old young men. Every season I get one year older and the team remains the same age! I don't declare the proverbial "get off my lawn" to Generation Z, but instead, offer to share the lawn....with the understanding that it's still MY lawn!

Digital technology is a convenient educational resource, has vastly improved worldwide communication, and has decreased the attention span of today's players. The two-inch by five-inch device (give or take an inch or two) that consumes Generation Z is commonly referred to as a cell phone. However, the more appropriate description is a cellular device because Generation Z has their nose pointed at the screen in text mode far more than they have their "magic square" pinned to their ear as a phone. The addiction to cellular devices has created a more impersonal world, especially for Generation Z.

An existence minus face-to-face communication decreases attention span. On our first road trip of the season, I splurge and take our squad to a nice restaurant for a team meal. No cell phones allowed at dinner is the rule, and all cell phones are confiscated before we enter the restaurant. I thoroughly enjoy observing our players socially interact with each other minus their cell phones. Once we depart the restaurant our players resemble crack addicts as they scurry to retrieve their cell phones. Several years ago my eyes were really opened when I was making a recruiting call and left a voicemail message for a prospect. The prospect immediately texted me after I had called with this message, "Hey coach I saw you called. What's up?" My impulsive thought was, "Why don't you answer your damn phone so we can have a human conversation and talk about 'what's up'?!" This game of technological hide and seek is commonplace for recruiters and illustrates the text addiction. I have an exercise for you that will validate my bitch session regarding cellular devices relative to decreased attention span. The next time you attend a Major League game pick a section of spectators. Tabulate how many are glued to their magic square, and how many are without a cellular device. The Magic Square always wins and usually by a landslide! I'm saddened to see a family of four's relationship stunted because they are jointly sidetracked by their magic squares. Nothing like shelling out 500 bucks for parking, concessions, and a game nobody watches!

"Time on task" is a phrase I initially heard during an Education class at Missouri Western and it has stuck with me my entire career. "Time on task" is the percentage of time a person spends during preparation for their chosen sport, occupation, hobby, etc. I measure "time on task" to govern every phase of our baseball program. Unfortunately, "time **off** task" during preparation impedes the progress of many organizations. The staff meeting in most instances is the ultimate example of "time off task." I bet you have experienced this waste of time at some point in your life: A leader interrupts their entire organization's production to have a staff meeting that accomplishes absolutely nothing. Unlike the aforementioned one-hour documentary on The Hawk, staff meetings usually leave workers mumbling, "that's an hour of my life I'll never get back." College baseball coaches "time off task" mistakes include dedicating ample practice time to aspects of the game that rarely occur, team meetings, and in-game charts. Some coaches spend hours practicing their first and third defense for something that happens three to five times the entire season. I would rather dedicate 90% of our practice time to pitching, hitting, and defense which happens every single game on our schedule. Team meetings are Baseball's version of the staff meeting. Coaches considering a motivational in-season team meeting should choose their date wisely because team meetings are only as good as your next game's starting pitcher! I only keep four in-game charts and they all serve as useful resources. However, many baseball coaches have a fetish with in-game charts. They inundate bench players with a jillion charts that are never used. A pissed off player posing as a clipboard holder, and in some cases freezing his ass off, is a poster child for "time off task."

Identifying attention span deficit with Generation Z is a simple diagnosis. How to combat the issue is more complicated. I cannot magically lengthen the attention span of a generation that has been trained to focus in short doses, but I can create a plan built on short-term vision. I strategically design our practice plans to maintain a high level of "time on task" during Generation Z's preparation. Our practices never exceed two and a half hours. A shorter organized practice is more beneficial than a longer practice that is filled with "time off task." A practice plan is a coach's time-based itinerary for that day's activities, but impromptu adjustments should be made if necessary. My practice plan is used more as a guide than a rigid schedule. For example, if 3:30 to 3:50 is designated for bunt defense, we will definitely finish the drill at 3:50 or earlier. I will revisit our bunt defense at a practice in the near future if throwing the baseball resembles a bad snowball fight. Coaches with a "we're going to get this right if it takes all day" mentality cause self-induced hypertension, and fail to recognize Generation Z's attention span deficit. Former heavyweight boxing champion Mike Tyson once said, "Everyone has a plan until they get punched in the mouth." Iron Mike's words are prophetic in describing practice plans!

Pitchers and defenders typically have ten to twenty-five seconds between pitches (dependent on the pitcher's pace) to prepare themselves for the pitcher's next delivery. "Only one thing grows in your hand" is an old saying at the poker table chastising a slow-paced player that can't decide which card to play. I apply the same mindset to pitching, and require our hurlers to work at a ten to twelve-second pace. A brisk pace allows their mind to remain uncluttered and their defense to stay sharp. A pitching staff will throw approximately 120 pitches per nine-inning game. Therefore, players must have a focused attention span 120 separate times to perform at peak level. The pitcher and catcher can't have an attention span lapse because they are obviously involved every pitch. We challenge our other seven defenders to lock in every pitch and **expect** every pitch to be hit to them. Our third baseman can lock in for 119 out of 120 pitches and **NOT** have a baseball hit to him, but the one pitch out of 120 he takes off could be a game-deciding defensive play. I explain this mental tug of war with our players, emphasize the importance of locking in every pitch, and constantly use the phrase "every pitch is a new game" as a reminder. In-game attention span deficit is especially prevalent when a player deals with failure. Pay close attention to a defensive player after he strikes out with runners in scoring position. Let's use Player A as an example. The scene will look something like this:

* Player A dejectedly trots to his defensive position with shoulders slumped and head down.

* Player A spends the defensive inning with hands on knees and head down between pitches, or takes phantom swings between pitches while still pondering his failed at-bat.

* Player A takes the defensive inning completely off. His team should pray to the Baseball Gods that a baseball is not hit to Player A because it's tough to see with your head lodged in your ass!

I certainly don't claim victory in the battle of Munns vs. The Magic Square, but I'm standing toe-to-toe, and furiously counter punching, to reach the next round/ generation!

Why are some people more competitive than others? Research suggests we are all born with a competitive gene. I commend scientists' efforts that have made the world a better place, and would be foolish to argue that genetics does not play a role in a person's competitive spirit. After all, I earned a D in General Biology and lack a scientist's IQ credentials, but I am 100% certain a player's competitiveness is a byproduct of their upbringing. I cut my competitive teeth playing cards, marbles, and checkers with my Grandmother. She never took it easy on her grandson, and she strictly enforced one post-game rule. Win or lose I was required to shake hands with her and say, "good game." The lessons learned in competitiveness and sportsmanship on the kitchen table in my Grandmother's farmhouse has served as my foundation for a lifetime in Athletics. I have carried on the family tradition two generations later by making Mary Ellen Munns earn her *Uno* and *Go Fish* victories over her father, and I still mandate the post-game handshake! Cheers to Baseball and Grandma Berger! Generation Z is **collectively** less competitive than past generations. I highlighted the word "**collectively**" so some players, parents, and coaches aren't offended. I have had the privilege to coach numerous Generation Z players that are fierce competitors, and their generation is irrelevant to their competitive spirit. Parents should support their children. Children should love their parents. Parents and children should disconnect during the athletic experience. A helicopter parent describes a parent that hovers over their child's athletic experience which severely stunts their child's competitive spirit, and is a pain in the ass for the coach. Breastfeeding provides healthy nourishment for an infant, and is a natural bond between mother and child. Many Generation Z players never figuratively get off the "titty milk," and thus are less competitive due to relying on Mom and Dad as a crutch. ESPN recently aired "The Last Dance," which is a 10-hour documentary starring basketball icon Michael Jordan. Michael's mother, Deloris Jordan, told viewers she advised Michael to work harder when he was cut from his high school basketball team. The birth of MJ's renowned competitiveness, which was on full display during "The Last Dance," can be attributed to his Mom. The competitive spirit of Generation Z would dramatically improve if helicopters were replaced with parents like Mrs. Jordan!

Coaches can also serve as enablers for zapping the competitive juices from Generation Z. I vote for the participation trophy to join the golden toad and dodo bird on the extinct species list. The popular practice of youth sports awarding a trophy to all participants eliminates the spirit of competition. Losing teaches valuable lessons while serving as a motivator, and should not be celebrated with a glorified handout. I witnessed the barrage of gifts the first time I accompanied my brother to watch my niece and nephew's high school cross country meet. The meet was over and the PA announcer declared the medal ceremony would begin in ten minutes.

My brother said, "Time to hit the road Bro before that gets started."

I replied, "I don't mind sticking around to show respect to the winners."

My brother looked at me like I had three heads and informed me, "The top **100** runners receive medals and it will take over an hour."

I quickly agreed to depart the course before the medal-palooza ensued. I have tremendous admiration for cross country athletes for their physical condition, dedication, and grit. However, rewarding the 100th best performer is ludicrous, and I wonder if the master of ceremonies congratulated runner number 100 for being slow! Nick Saban, Alabama's Head Football Coach, won his seventh national title after the Crimson Tide bludgeoned Ohio State 52-24 in the 2020 College Football National Championship Game. After the game, Coach Saban offered this reply while being interviewed, "You heard me say before, I hate to lose. And I don't care how much you win, you still hate to lose. And you can talk about the seven that we've won, but the two that haunt me are the two that we lost. Don't ask me why it's that way." Coach Saban's mentality is a driving force for his unparalleled success, and participation trophies gifted to Generation Z will not create the next Nick Saban.

Generation Z could have just as easily been labeled Generation Reboot. The evolution of the computer made "reboot" a popular term, and starting over became a quick fix to resume activity. Today's college athletes' version of pressing the on/off button is transferring to another school. I would be hypocritical by blindly criticizing transfers because I transferred myself as a student-athlete, and have benefited my entire coaching career by recruiting transfers. Every place is not for everybody! There are a multitude of legitimate reasons that student-athletes search for greener pastures elsewhere; including unexpected financial loss, family hardship, philosophical differences with the coach, and switching academic majors. Sadly, being allergic to competition has become the primary reason for players rebooting to another school. They would rather transfer than attempt beating out a teammate of equal or more ability. The NCAA succumbed to Generation Reboot's desires by loosening transfer rules, and creating the transfer portal which debuted on October 15, 2018. The transfer portal is a website that is a centralized database for players interested in transferring. A player simply enters his name in the portal, and they are accessible to coaches from every NCAA school. The transfer portal is bursting at the seams with over a thousand baseball players entered during the summer of 2020. The NCAA has created a transfer monster that is like catching fish in a barrel for recruiters.

I recommend recruiters beware because the whopper you hook may actually be a minnow in disguise if they lack competitiveness!

Most people immediately think of profanity when they hear the phrase "four-letter word." In Athletics, the most demeaning and insulting four-letter word is not profane, but spelled Q U I T. A true competitor NEVER quits regardless of the odds stacked against them. Webster's defines "compete" as "striving to gain or win something by defeating or establishing superiority over others who are trying to do the same." An extra level of com-petitiveness is required when you are equal to your opponent or the underdog. We are all guilty of unknowingly leaving competitive fuel in our tank. The widget is an age-old fictitious product used to illustrate a person's competitive tank. Two employees perform the exact same task in the workplace. One employee produces 1,000 widgets during the workday, and the other employee produces 500 widgets during the workday. Both employees go home feeling equally tired even though one worked twice as hard as the other. My challenge is to maximize Generation Z's widget production. Quite simply, daily emphasis is the key to instilling competitiveness. I refer back to bullet point number seven in The Cougar Way, "Practice like you play in your biggest game (focus, energy, **competitiveness**)." "Old school" coaches make the mistake of comparing current players' competitiveness to themselves or past generations. The only comparison I care about is our team vs. our opponents. Our Generation Z has to be more competitive than their Generation Z!

Baseball has undergone a major facelift in recent years, and all three phases of the game have been impacted (defense, hitting, pitching). Technology, analytics, and revamped training methods have been instrumental in changing the game during Generation Z. Ivy League whiz kids have replaced veteran baseball lifers as Major League general managers, a computer decides game strategy instead of human eyeballs, and today's players are trained strictly for power at the plate and on the mound. MLB teams previously employed **ONE** advance scout to prepare their ball club for upcoming opponents. The advance scout's job description is studying opponents' tendencies, styles, strengths, weaknesses, and reporting any other observation that could help their employer gain an advantage to win a baseball game. Advance scouts travel one city ahead of the team, and prepare a detailed scouting report that awaits the coaching staff upon arrival for their next opponent. Teams now employ analytic **DEPART-MENTS** that spend endless hours poring over computer-ized data and video. The tireless efforts of analytic experts, many of whom have never worn a jock strap, dictate organizational strategies and philosophies. I strongly believe today's black and white analytics, and "old school" human instincts, can co-exist. The area of the game most dramatically impacted is defensive positioning. "Defensive shift" is a phrase popularized by teams overloading one side of the field (usually the pull side) based on a hitter's history of where he hits the baseball. Exaggerated defensive shifts include positioning three infielders on one side of the field, and even employing four outfielders vs. a hitter with an extremely high fly ball rate. The left-handed pull hitter has suffered more than anybody due to defensive shifting. They face a defensive alignment with no third baseman, the shortstop shaded up the middle, the second baseman at regular depth, and the third baseman parked in short rightfield...but shallow enough to throw out a batter that hits him a ground ball. The SOB stationed in short rightfield is a lefty pull hitter's nemesis, and has turned yesteryear's singles into outs.

Why doesn't the lefty pull hitter push a bunt to the vacated third base position? Why doesn't the lefty pull hitter learn to hit the outside pitch to left field? Old Schoolers lose their minds watching hitters ignore these two glaring options, but today's game philosophizes that swinging for the fences is ALWAYS the best option. Nike aired a 1999 commercial in the midst of Baseball's Steroid Era that starred Atlanta Braves pitchers Greg Maddux and Tom Glavine, St. Louis Cardinals slugger Mark McGwire, and model/actress Heather Locklear. Maddux's signature line, "chicks dig the long ball," was a national phenomenon and propelled Nike cross-fit shoes to record sales. Due to the current love affair with home runs, I recommend that Nike should strongly consider a sequel to the "chicks dig the long ball" commercial. I'll let Nike recast who they want to replace Maddux, Glavine, McGwire, and Ms. Locklear. My only request is concluding the sequel with Bartolo Colon delivering the signature catchphrase, "chicks dig the long ball," accompanied by a replay of his one and only career home run. Why Bartolo Colon? Bartolo is a lovable, hefty, ageless wonder that pitched in the big leagues until he was 45 years old and won 247 games. However, his lone dinger at age 42, and subsequent home run trot/waddle that took him 30.6 seconds to round the bases, might be the most unlikely play in MLB history. 20 + years later, Nike could transform "chicks dig the long ball" into "chicks dig Bartolo!"

I'm quite certain Bartolo prescribed to "see ball hit ball" philosophy, or maybe even "close eyes and swing hard" philosophy, and was oblivious to the phrase "launch angle." Launch angle rules today's game, and is defined as the vertical angle, measured in degrees, of the baseball leaving a hitter's bat after being struck. In laymen's terms, hitters are being taught to lift the baseball which produces more balls in the air, and thus increases the probability for more home runs. I am stubborn to embrace the launch angle rage, but have implemented defensive shifting and modern pitcher training advancements into our program. Two out of three ain't bad for an "old school" college baseball coach! There are several problems with the launch angle hitting philosophy. A diverse team-oriented offensive approach enhances run production vs. good pitching. It's challenging to beat a really good pitcher when all nine hitters in the lineup are working as individuals, and the sole goal for each hitter is to launch the baseball into orbit. I still value hitters that are pests who work the count, bunt for a hit, and can handle the bat as situational hitters. I also value hitters that possess the power to change a game's outcome with one swing of their bat. The ability to teach two polar opposite offensive approaches, and have them coexist in the same lineup, enhances a team's offensive efficiency. There are premeditated productive outs that are major factors in winning games when an offense works as a cohesive unit. A hitter in our program is applauded for hitting a ground ball to a middle infielder, which scores a runner from third base with less than two outs. The late great Hank Aaron was once asked what he was most proud of as an offensive player. He replied, "Getting runners home from third base with less than two outs." The man nicknamed "Hammer" knocked in more runs than anybody in the history of Major League Baseball (2,297), and didn't need launch angle measurements to place second on MLB's career home run list (755). Hammerin' Hank's batting resume speaks for itself, but as impressive was the fact that he played twenty-four seasons and NEVER spent a day on the disabled list. If situational hitting is good enough for Hank Aaron, I'd like to think it is good enough for Generation Z's players! Henry Louis Aaron was beloved by all, and for my money is the most underrated player in baseball history.

The launch angle craze has sadly trickled down to college and high school baseball. Major League Baseball is comprised of grown men, many of whom are built like a linebacker, that are capable of hitting for power. Some college hitters (depending on the level), and very few high school hitters, possess the power to prescribe exclusively to the launch angle philosophy. Amateur coaches watch MLB and assume since power is king at the highest level then they should follow suit. Why coaches teach physically immature amateur players to launch the baseball is beyond me. Brace yourself for my greatest head-shaking launch angle story. I recently walked into our off-campus indoor hitting facility which is open to the public. A young lad had a batting tee elevated up to his neck, and was swinging straight upward, hitting baseballs directly into the top of the batting cage. The player informed me it was a launch angle drill that his personal hitting coach taught him. I couldn't resist telling the player that practicing popping out to the catcher is not a wise strategy to becoming a successful hitter. I hope for his sake he wasn't paying his personal hitting coach big dough to learn an exercise in futility. Another ingredient in the launch angle philosophy is making the strikeout acceptable for hitters. A two-strike approach used to mean hitters shortened up their swing, expanded the strike zone, and battled their ever-loving ass off to make contact. Today's two-strike approach is KEEP SWINGING FROM YOUR ASS, and it's perfectly fine if the at-bat ends in strike three. What has the offensive world come to when strikeouts are condoned and young players are being "coached" to pop out to the catcher!

The art of pitching a baseball is a combination of accuracy, body coordination, deception, stamina, and velocity. The final attribute on the aforementioned list (known as "velo" in baseball circles) is measured in miles per hour by a radar gun, and has always been coveted by pitchers. 90 used to be the magic number that indicated a hurler had arrived as a flame thrower, but 100 has replaced 90 as the velocity benchmark in today's game. The velocity revolution is clearly evident to anybody paying attention to Major League Baseball. Most pitchers, especially relievers, are registering velocity readings north of 95 miles per hour, and it's common to see triple digits. Velocity training, and the obsession with throwing a baseball as hard as humanly possible, has a stranglehold on the game. "Weighted balls" is a common phrase understood by everybody in today's game, and is at the forefront of the velocity spike happening in Baseball. A baseball weighs 5.25 ounces, and arm strength has always been developed by repeatedly throwing a 5.25-ounce baseball on a daily basis. Weighted ball programs consist of six to ten color-coded balls that range in weight from three ounces to four pounds. The number of balls incorporated, and weights of each ball, vary depending on each individual program. Most of the balls, with the exception of the heaviest balls, are roughly the size of a baseball. Pitchers train by throwing the balls into a plyo board, or plyo wall, designed to withstand the constant pounding of the weighted balls. The basic concept of overloading and underloading the throwing process increases arm speed, and therefore translates to increased velocity. Weighted balls used to be waterlogged baseballs that were accidentally left out in the rain, and now they are a cluster of balls resembling Easter eggs that build 100 mile per hour arms!

Over the course of time, a pitcher's level of activity in the weight room has evolved from non-existent to an addictive daily regimen. Yesteryear's pitchers were often skinny, dumpy, or "country strong." The vast majority of today's pitchers are wound tight, and built like cartoon characters. Quite simply, a powerful pitcher delivers a more powerful fastball. The hyphenated term risk-reward was originally used as the ratio that measured how much money investors risked to how much money they could be potentially rewarded. The maniacal pursuit of velocity by coaches and pitchers works in reverse order of the popular investment model, and places the reward before the risk. Weighted ball programs and aggressive strength training definitely increase the odds of a velocity spike for pitchers, but they also dramatically increase the risk for injury. It is not coincidental that velocity and surgeries are both at an all-time high in high school, college, and professional baseball. Baseball is training pitchers for power, but in many cases disregards durability and longevity. In the sport of drag racing, cars cover a quarter of a mile, reach speeds of up to 335 miles per hour, and deploy a parachute from the ass-end of the car so they can hopefully come to a safe stop. Baseball is asking dragsters (pitchers) to race in the Daytona 500 while still sticking their speedometer on 335! Enjoy watching a powerful arm because eventually, it's probably going to break. Is it possible to achieve increased velocity and maintain durability?

The first step for pitching coaches, when tackling the velocity/durability equation, is to realize that pitching a baseball is not a healthy activity, and comes with inherent injury risk. The overhand throwing motion is unnatural for human beings. We don't walk around with our arms over our heads like an orangutan because it is unnatural. It is obviously more natural to walk around with dangling arms, and our hands below our waist. For this reason, softball pitchers are extremely durable and can pitch every day. College softball pitching staffs consist of two or three pitchers that gobble up all of their team's innings for the entire season. A college baseball pitching staff is a unit of 15-20 arms because baseball pitchers require more rest between outings, and are more susceptible to injuries, especially when delivering the baseball with more velocity than ever before. Tommy John pitched in the big leagues for 26 seasons and ranks seventh among left-handed pitchers with 288 career wins. However, despite an illustrious Major League career, the name Tommy John is synonymous with elbow surgery for today's players. In 1974 Dr. Frank Jobe made Mr. John the guinea pig as the first baseball player to undergo ulnar collateral ligament (UCL) surgery, which became universally known as Tommy John surgery. The surgical procedure replaces the UCL (located in the elbow) with another tendon from the pitcher's body (other elbow, calf, etc.). A tendon from a corpse can also be used for the procedure. I have zero medical background, but I would request the UCL from Bob Gibson, Walter Johnson, or Bob Feller. Why not take your chances acquiring the UCL from a deceased flame throwing MLB legend, such as Gibby, The Big Train, or Bullet Bob! Tommy John surgery, known as TJ to the Baseball community, has become a routine procedure. Hurlers adorning zipper-like scars on their pitching elbows usually come back stronger than they were before the surgery. The extremely resilient persevere through multiple Tommy John surgeries and keep on pitching! An experimental surgery by Dr. Jobe in 1974 has provided a security blanket for pitchers hell-bent on increasing velocity, drastically changed the course of Baseball history, and made Tommy John a household name.

Here is the answer to the previously posed million-dollar question: Increased velocity and durability can co-exist, but a diligent plan is mandatory to satisfy both agendas. Unfortunately, the love affair coaches have with velocity usually takes complete precedent, and keeps UCL surgeons in high demand. My "old school" mentality, and a career spent successfully developing pitchers, were factors in me being late to the weighted balls party. Tyler Anderson motivated me to finally incorporate weighted balls into our pitching program. Tyler was a right-handed pitcher that I recruited to play at William Woods. After a stellar collegiate career, Tyler played professionally in Australia, coached college baseball at several schools, and is currently a pitching coach in the Philadelphia Phillies organization. Tyler began studying weighted balls while playing in Australia, and eventually created his own arm care program, which was instrumental in his rise from William Woods to professional baseball. Tyler continuously urged me to implement his arm care program because he genuinely cared about the success of our program, and I continually declined his offering. I was guilty of being apprehensive to change my proven process, and connect with Generation Z. The old stubborn jackass named Coach Munns finally relented in 2018, thanks to Boomer and Tyler convincing me weighted balls could be **added** to our pitching program, and not **replace** our pitching program. This jackass is pleased to report that our pitching program has benefited from using weighted balls. Cheers to Baseball and Tyler Anderson!

The problem with amateur baseball is there are too many pitching trainers, and not enough pitching coaches. The pitching trainer has velo on the brain at all times, and he judges a pitcher strictly by digits on a radar gun. A pitching coach understands that velocity is an important piece of the pitching puzzle, but not the only piece. Sadly, irresponsible pitching trainers make a pretty penny preying on youngsters seeking a magical velo spike. Amateur pitchers become addicted to weighted balls when they see velocity gains, and crave more weighted balls. The "More is Better" philosophy is a recipe for disaster when pitchers train with weighted balls. Studies show drinking a daily glass of red wine is healthy, but drinking two bottles of wine is a headache waiting to happen. A prescribed dose of weighted balls improves velocity, but overdosing on weighted balls results in a snapped ulnar collateral ligament. Velocity is a helpful additive, but useless if the man on the bump can't throw strikes, or lacks competitive spirit. Adam Wainwright is nearing the end of his decorated Major League career as a right-handed pitcher with the St. Louis Cardinals that began in 2005. Waino has led the league in wins twice, pitched in All Star Games, and recorded the last out of the Cardinals 2006 World Series Championship. However, in my opinion his greatest accomplishment is succeeding in today's game at age 40, while possessing a fastball that frequently registers under 90 miles per hour. He is truly a pitching oddity as a soft righty in 2020! Father Time has stripped Wainwright of Major League velocity, but he continues to win because he knows how to pitch and he is the ultimate competitor. For every Adam Wainwright, there are 100 pitchers toiling in the minor leagues with electric arms that can't figure it out. Waino confidently stomps around the mound with an "I'm here to kick your ass" look in his eyes despite operating with a pedestrian fastball. I'm an old school college baseball coach that has connected with Generation Z by embracing weighted balls. I also thoroughly enjoy watching the velo-challenged Mr. Wainwright win games using brains, guts, and a GIANT set of nuts!

I was inherently blessed with an extremely strong competitive gene that was even further fueled by Grandma Berger, Coach Scanlon, and Don Maines. While researching how to write a book, I discovered that 97% of all first-time aspiring authors never finish their book. Challenge accepted! I don't know if *Cheers to Baseball* will be a New York Times bestseller or merely a keepsake for Mary Ellen Munns, but Yours Truly joining the 3% was an absolute lock! My competitive drive is the primary reason I flipped four college baseball programs from non-existent/laughingstocks into improbable winners. I take great pride in my competitiveness, but ultimately I compete vicariously through our players and they determine my fate. "Old school" coaches either connect with younger generations or their careers die quicker than Joseph "Blue" Pulaski in a pool of KY jelly! Thanks for taking the time to read my book. Cheers to Baseball and You!

# Acknowledgements

I could have never written *Cheers to Baseball* without the initial backing of my parents who fully supported my love for the game of Baseball as a youngster. They provided a glove for my hand every little league season, gifted me a box of Topps baseball cards for every one of my birthdays, and my Dad made sure I knew Bob Gibson was the baddest man that ever stepped on a baseball field. Don Maines is my mentor in college baseball, and I am forever grateful that he took a shot on a clueless first-year assistant coach. My career, ability to lead others, and *Cheers to Baseball* would not be possible without his tutelage. I also acknowledge a select group of readers that took time from their busy schedules to provide candid feedback one chapter at a time to a first-time author. Cheers to Baseball and the following readers:

Tim Brandow
Mary Eisele
Roy Hallenbeck
Greg Hill
John Houf
Jason Immekus
Mark Jordan
Eric Mason
Craig McAndrews

Eric Moore
Mike Morhardt
David Munns
Sarah Munns
Anne Rogers
Steve Torricelli
Tim Torricelli

Craig "Boomer" McAndrews has been with me for nearly two decades as a player and assistant coach. Boomer is much more than an assistant coach to me, and deserves special mention for his loyalty, dedication, and friendship. I also acknowledge every other assistant coach that has ever served on one of my coaching staffs. Chapter Five is titled "Great People = Great Results," and the great people that served as my assistant coaches are the reason we achieved great results. The following individuals listed either volunteered, or were paid far less than their efforts, to make our programs better. Their love of the game, and willingness to go the extra mile, greatly impacted countless young men. These names may not mean anything to you, but they mean everything to me.

Patrick Anderson
Caleb Bounds
Jordan Dey
Colby Fitch
Chris Fletcher
Shane Herschelman
Andy Hight
Gavin Jones
Alex Kazmierski

Bob Kern
Mike Kern
Brian Myers
Matt Sissom
Jim Smetzer
Zac Stokes
Tim Stunkel
Josh Swenson
Tanner Williamson

Last, but certainly not least, I acknowledge and thank my supportive wife, Sarah, for her unwavering support during this project. She is ecstatic I have completed the book so she doesn't have to answer my continuous pondering, "What do you think of _____ for my book?" An author's wife, like a coach's wife, is a special person. Sarah Munns now qualifies as both. Sarah is definitely Heaven-bound for her tolerance of Yours Truly. Saint Peter will grant her royal treatment, and ask everybody in line at the Pearly Gates to please step aside upon her arrival!

# About Atmosphere Press

Atmosphere Press is an independent, full-service publisher for excellent books in all genres and for all audiences. Learn more about what we do at atmospherepress.com.

We encourage you to check out some of Atmosphere's latest releases, which are available at Amazon.com and via order from your local bookstore:

*The Swing: A Muse's Memoir About Keeping the Artist Alive,* by Susan Dennis

*Possibilities with Parkinson's: A Fresh Look,* by Dr. C

*Gaining Altitude - Retirement and Beyond,* by Rebecca Milliken

*Out and Back: Essays on a Family in Motion,* by Elizabeth Templeman

*Just Be Honest,* by Cindy Yates

*You Crazy Vegan: Coming Out as a Vegan Intuitive,* by Jessica Ang

*Detour: Lose Your Way, Find Your Path,* by S. Mariah Rose

*To B&B or Not to B&B: Deromanticizing the Dream,* by Sue Marko

*Convergence: The Interconnection of Extraordinary Experiences,* by Barbara Mango and Lynn Miller

*Sacred Fool,* by Nathan Dean Talamantez

*My Place in the Spiral,* by Rebecca Beardsall

*My Eight Dads,* by Mark Kirby

*Eat to Lead,* by Luci Gabel

CPSIA information can be obtained
at www.ICGtesting.com
Printed in the USA
LVHW021624150622
721324LV00005B/778

9 781639 882465